Craft

Gideon's Way

ISBN   0-85116-585-0

Features

£3.99

Complete Story By SHEILA LEWIS

A DAY OUT
LOND

4

IN ON

It was a super prize he won but it was his escorts who were the real winners — if only they could see it!

T HE file, Miss Amery," Robert Andrews said wearily. "Just send me the file, all the details will be available to me then."

"Yes, but I think I ought to explain —" Her voice at the other end of the line sounded anxious.

"Look, Miss Amery, I know Mr Croft has been handling this account, but I can quite easily grasp all the facts. I don't need chapter and verse, just their names and time of arrival."

There was a slight pause. "Very well, Mr Andrews. Johnson and Taylor, Waterloo, 10 a.m. I *do* hope you enjoy your day." There was no mistaking the sarcasm in Miss Amery's voice.

Robert replaced the receiver with a sigh. He knew he'd been sharp with Miss Amery, but after all, this was supposed to be his day off.

He should have been spending today on a yacht, rocking gently in some sheltered harbour miles away from London. Justine's uncle's yacht. He smiled, thinking of Justine.

But Miss Amery had telephoned to say that Mr Croft had gone down to the factory of his latest clients — the new toothpaste account — where there had been a serious fire. Naturally Mr Croft couldn't meet these two people as planned, so Robert had to stand in for him.

He consulted his watch. Surely he could cope with this meeting in under an hour? He telephoned Justine to say so. "I'll be a little late, darling, that's all."

"Not too late, Robert, my love, or else I shall have to travel down

5

with Simon." Her tone was honey sweet and ice cold.

"I'll be there," he said grimly.

A messenger brought the file to him half an hour later and he glanced at it briefly. The new toothpaste account; no need to delve into it, he'd already discussed the most important issues with Mr Croft.

He reached Waterloo by 9.50 a.m. and left a message at the station for Messrs Taylor and Johnston to meet him in the coffee lounge nearby. It was quiet and subdued with an air of studied elegance. He ordered coffee and unfolded his paper.

A few minutes later the waitress approached him.

"Excuse me, Mr Andrews. Someone to see you."

Robert looked up.

"Over there by the door." She pointed.

Lowering his paper, Robert looked in the direction of the door, where a girl and a young boy stood looking round hopefully.

"Are you sure they asked for me?" he said to the waitress.

" 'Course I am. You left a message for them to meet you here."

"Oh . . . thanks." Robert rose hurriedly from the table.

The girl by the door had seen their conversation and was now threading her way through the tables, with the boy in tow.

"Mr Andrews?" She smiled a wide, delighted smile. "Hello, how nice to meet you. I'm Sally Johnson."

She took his hand and shook it enthusiastically. Then she drew the boy forward and stood with her hands on his shoulders, beaming over his head at Robert.

"And this is the person you've been waiting for — Tommy Taylor!"

"Er, hello," Robert said, slightly stunned by the introduction.

"How do you do, Mr Andrews? I'm very pleased to meet you." They shook hands. The boy was neatly dressed and immaculately scrubbed and shining.

"He's so excited, Mr Andrews. I hope you don't mind that I've come along in place of my sister, Tommy's mother — on account of the twins, you see. But you got my letter, of course?"

"Er — well — not exactly. I'm standing in for Mr Croft — you see . . . ." Robert stammered to a halt, taking in for the first time the girl's honey complexion, shining fair hair and delicate and delightful perfume.

BUT he hadn't the faintest idea what she was talking about. Obviously this was no ordinary conversation with two clients. Robert groaned silently. If only he hadn't been dreaming of Justine and a day on the rippling waters of the Solent . . .

They were looking at him in puzzlement, obviously expecting something. He racked his brains and switched on a smile.

"Coffee and . . . ice-cream?" he asked.

"Oh, yes please!" Tommy said enthusiastically.

Robert ordered, then excused himself. "I'll have to telephone my office, keep in touch — there's a crisis, you see. Shan't be a moment."

He fled from the table, and into the telephone booth at the entrance to the lounge he surreptitiously extracted the file from his briefcase.

He read through it with a sinking heart. Of course — the competition. How could he have forgotten? Croft had thought up a schools contest to name the new brand.

Tommy Taylor's name had been drawn out of the hat to represent the winning school. The last letter in the file said his mother had just had twins, so his aunt would accompany him to London.

No wonder Miss Amery had tried so hard to warn him about this "meeting." But what was this?

With mounting horror, Robert read that Tommy and his aunt were to be taken on a tour of the toothpaste factory and premises, with lunch in the staff dining-room. That was certainly out, after the fire. Relief flooded through him. With any luck that would be that. A polite apology, rearrange the date of the tour, and he might yet have his day with Justine as planned.

He returned to the table with the apologetic smile at the ready.

"I'm terribly sorry, Tommy, but we've had a bit of a disaster today." He explained about the fire. "So I'm afraid a tour of our premises is out." He shook his head sadly at Miss Johnson.

"Oh, what a pity!" She looked downcast, but only for a moment. "Where can you take us instead?"

"Take you?" Robert said faintly.

"Look, Mr Andrews —" The girl's voice was eager. "Tommy's never been to London before. Could we just be tourists? You could show us some of London's landmarks."

If there was anything Robert loathed, it was the tourist trip. He glanced at his watch.

"Can we go to the Tower — where the princes died?" Tommy asked.

"Oh yes, please!" Sally put an enthusiastic hand on Robert's arm. "We could see the very spot where Anne Boleyn was beheaded. You must think we're a ghoulish pair, Mr Andrews, but honestly we've read so much history that to see the actual places would make it all come alive — so to speak."

Robert resigned himself to the inevitable. An afternoon wasted in a trip round the Tower — and Justine gone without him. He remembered Simon, and had to stop himself from grinding his teeth.

"I think we can manage that, Miss Johnson," he said magnanimously.

A lovely smile from Sally Johnson was his reward. She was really quite attractive in an unspoilt way, he thought. Not his type, of course, Justine was quite different — beautiful, smooth as silk. She wouldn't be seen in the Tower — dead or alive.

Sally rose from the table, and turned to him hesitantly.

"I say, isn't all this Mister and Miss a bit formal? I'm Sally."

Continued on page 10.

Take A Handful

... and you'll discover that, whether you add them to the cookpot or plant them in the garden, their versatility is boundless!

IF anyone asked me if I grew herbs, I might very well reply by saying:

"It depends on what you mean by herbs." There are so many kinds.

Lavender and Lad's Love are herbs, but I only ever grow them as flowering plants that smell nice. Marigolds and nasturtiums are widely grown for their colourful flowers, but marigold petals can be used as a flavouring. Nasturtium leaves can be eaten, whereas mint and sage are grown simply for kitchen use.

Really, herbs are plants whose leaves, stems or seeds contain aromatic oils.

So, having sorted that out, let's have a closer look at the herbs that are really useful for everyday needs. These are the kind that give special flavours to food.

IT is best to decide exactly what space you have available and then grow only those herbs for which you have a constant use.

Be wary of things like mint and horseradish, as once they start growing they never know when to stop.

Mint is better in a border by itself and horseradish needs to be banished to a faraway place to rampage on its own. I don't know which of the two would win if they were placed together. I've never tried that!

I think it's better to grow perennials only in one place, and annuals, if wanted, separately. Useful low-growing perennial herbs are chives,

thyme, sage, garlic and parsley. Annuals you might like are summer savory, borage, sweet marjoram and basil.

If I could only grow one herb it would be chives. It's a neat plant and I grow mine as an edging to a bed. I've also grown it in pots successfully.

The slender, tubular leaves have a mild onion flavour and chopped up are delicious in mixed salads or with cottage cheese, scrambled egg. And they're a "must" in potato salad.

It has pretty pink flowers like Thrift. Chives do best in a good soil and don't mind a little shade.

Thyme is a compact plant and the golden-leaved lemon-scented variety is really attractive. It's fine, used sparingly, for flavouring any sort of meat or with vegetables. When growing, it likes a dry sunny place.

Sage is prettily grey leaved and with onion makes a stuffing for pork. Parsley makes a good sauce, with fish and is nice to have for garnishing all kinds of dishes.

Garlic cloves are easy to grow if you really like them, but they do need a good rich soil to encourage them.

Chives, thyme and sage can be bought as small plants from most garden shops, as can cloves of garlic. Parsley can be grown from seed, but it can be very slow to germinate.

NOW for the annuals, all of which can be grown from seed. Summer savoury is sharp

Of Herbs

By FLORENCE BASTIE

tasting and useful in stuffings. Bees love its pink flowers.

Borage is a delightful plant and not fussy as to position, also loved by bees. I like the leaves, which have a slight cucumber flavour, chopped in salad, or you can float a sprig in cool summer drinks. You can also have the vivid blue flowers in a pot-pourri.

Many gardeners grow nasturtiums, but I wonder how many have ever eaten the leaves. I just like to chew one. They are hot and peppery, so one or two are fine in a salad.

Sweet marjoram likes to grow in a sunny spot. It has a spicy taste and is particularly good as a flavouring in sausages. Basil is clove scented and tasty with all tomato dishes. It prefers a sunny sheltered spot.

HERBS are not only for flavouring food, though that may be their main use. Many of them are really good for you. Parsley, for instance, is rich in Vitamin C; thyme helps the digestion of fats; and summer savoury and marjoram can replace salt.

Sweet Cicely is a unique hardy plant. It grows 2-3 ft. (60-90 cm) high and is really sweet and a sugar-saver. A few leaves added when stewing sour fruit such as rhubarb, gooseberries, blackcurrant and plums, add a piquant flavour and can save as much as half the sugar needed.

Its leaves are ready to pick as soon as they are fully developed. They are pretty in growth but not easy to dry, as they are so large.

If you want to dry herbs for winter use, gather them before the flowers open and spread them out in a cool oven, or tie into small bunches and hang them upside-down in an airy place. When the leaves are crisp to the touch, hand rub them and keep them in air-tight glass jars. □

A DAY OUT IN LONDON

Continued from page 7.

THE White Tower was a great success. Sally raved over the costumes, and Tommy turned out to be something of an authority on weapons — Robert was amazed at what he knew.

Personally, he'd had no idea that there was such a wide variety of treasures in the Tower.

It was almost noon when they finally left.

"Can we go back on a boat?" Tommy asked, heading for the pier.

"By all means," Robert agreed stonily.

Sally enthused over the view of the Tower and the bridge from the pleasure boat. "Look, Tommy — oh, Robert, the outlines against the sky! What impact; such terrific drama, don't you think?"

Robert glanced back and nodded thoughtfully. He'd seen the skyline of London day and night, dawn and dusk, for years.

Sally was watching him closely. "You don't mean to say you've got used to it?" she asked with disbelief in her voice.

Robert shrugged.

As the boat churned to Westminster Pier, Sally and Tommy didn't seem to mind the wind and the spray.

"Look at the bridge!"

"Did you know that part of Cleopatra's Needle has stone that is 5000 years old?"

The questions came thick and fast. Robert sat immobile and unresponsive in the centre of the boat. Eventually the voyage was over, the barker on the boat's public address finished his spiel, and they tied up at Westminster Pier.

"Now, I don't want to detain you —" Robert began, hoping fervently there was a train to their particular village within the next fifteen minutes.

"We haven't had our lunch!" Tommy pointed out with a certain degree of self-righteousness. "It's part of the prize."

"Tommy!" Sally was blushing. "I'm so sorry, Robert."

Mentally, Robert said goodbye to Justine.

"I completely forgot," he lied. "Where would you like to go for lunch?"

"Can we have sandwiches and crisps, and a drink from a can?" Tommy's eyes were alight with hope.

"Maybe we could go to a park and eat here." Sally looked at Robert.

"A park?" This was really getting out of hand.

Sally snapped her fingers. "Of course — St James's Park — then we can see the Palace too."

They purchased their picnic from the park's café, and found a spot near the lake so that the ducks could have their crusts.

Robert and Sally sat companionably under a tree, watching Tommy feeding the Canada geese and throwing crusts far out into the lake for the swans.

"I doubt if my firm would approve of this, Sally," he said. "You really should be lunching in a comfortable restaurant —"

"Oh no, Robert. We can have a meal in a restaurant any day. Just for today only, St James's Park is our restaurant. You've no idea how I envy you, living in London. It's so exciting, magical."

"What do you do with yourself in . . . Nerston Edge, is it?"

"Sounds like the end of the world, doesn't it?" She grinned. "But it isn't. It's alive with music and drama and sport and good works and — just like any other community, I suppose."

"Do you take part in *all* of those?"

"She sings and dances," Tommy told him proudly. "She's good, too."

"I'm a frustrated ballet dancer at heart." Her eyes became wistful. "I'd love to go to Covent Garden," she said. "Oh well, perhaps another time."

"I'm a keen opera lover," he told her. "Although I must confess I mostly listen to tapes and records."

"Don't you go to the performances?" Sally's eyes were wide with concern. "I wouldn't miss one!"

"Oh, well." He shrugged, and realised for the first time that no-one had ever wanted to accompany him. Justine only liked parties and socialising . . .

"Can we go to Madame Tussaud's now?" Tommy asked.

Robert groaned aloud and turned to Sally, but she was looking hopeful too.

The real attraction there was The Chamber of Horrors. Tommy inspected every scene in the darkened dungeon meticulously, but Robert was aware that Sally's bright voice was quiet and that she didn't move far away from him.

"Bit spooky for you?"

"Yes . . . atmospheric." Her voice was small and unsure, and he warmed to her uncertainty.

"Croft's Dental Care always looks after its customers," he said quietly, taking her small hand in his.

OUTSIDE, in the late sunshine, Sally looked up at him with a gentle smile on her face.

"It's been a wonderful day, Robert. Isn't London just marvellous?"

Robert looked into her big eyes, the eyes through which today he'd seen a new and exciting city, and swallowed. What on earth was happening to him?

Continued on page 15.

THERE'S A LONG, LONG

By EILEEN ELIAS

"Walk the Great Wall of China? You must be joking!" But Eileen Elias managed to convince her husband that it was too great a challenge to miss . . .

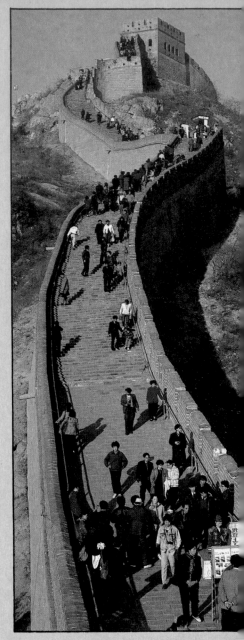

I'VE always been fascinated by walls. And when I think of those thousands of people who visit Hadrian's Wall every year, I don't think I can be the only one.

And think of the Great Wall of China. I've always had a secret longing to stand on top of that, ever since I first saw pictures of it snaking across two and a half thousand miles of mountains in the old "Children's Encyclopaedia" we had at home.

More recently, I discovered that the Wall is the only piece of man's handiwork that can be seen by astronauts on the Moon. And that clinched it for me. If ever I was to get to China.

Well, come the spring I did. Don't ask me how, but there we were, my long-suffering husband and I, stepping out of the plane into sunshine and peach-blossom at Peking Airport.

Naturally, the first thing I said to our guides was, "Can I go and climb the Great Wall?"

Our two black-haired, blue-suited guides, Mr Koo and Mr Wong, smiled simultaneously, showing two rows each of faultless white teeth.

"Of course," said Mr Koo.

"Everyone wants to see our Wall," said Mr Wong.

"When can I go?" I asked, ignoring my husband's frantic signalling. He likes walls — but just to look at. Climbing them is a different matter, and there's an awful lot of the Great Wall to climb.

"Next Sunday?" Mr Koo suggested.

"It will be our pleasure," Mr Wong added.

I was delighted. But how, I wondered, would we get there? I'd only been in China half an hour, and knew nothing about transport.

"By rickshaw?" I asked.

"No rickshaws now," Mr Koo said.

"By bicycle then?" In China people go everywhere by bicycle.

"Too far," Mr Koo said.

"How are we going, then?" I asked.

Mr Koo's smile and Mr Wong's smile beamed across their faces.

"We have a train. A brand-new train. With every comfort. It has only been on one run. You shall have special seats on the special train."

Surprise number one. I'd thought of China as an unsophisticated country — now, here it was with a spanking new train. And there I'd been, picturing myself setting out like some Everest explorer, gritting my teeth and thinking of England. It would all be quite easy after all.

Surprise number two was on the Sunday morning. I didn't know the Queen was coming to Peking. At least, who else could it be, since the streets to the station were lined three-deep with staring multitudes?

Hundreds upon hundreds of them: blue-suited Chinese fathers and mothers and grandparents, aunts and uncles and cousins and inumerable boys and girls with open mouths, and enchanting brown babies with black fringes above their wondering eyes. It must be the Queen.

But no, it wasn't. Mr Koo indicated the thronged streets. "They have come to see you off," he said.

"They like to see Westerners," Mr Wong added gallantly.

I blushed. But it was true. The crowds were indeed for us.

Once on that train, we settled down with a number of other Westerners to enjoy the experience and the scenery. While the radio greeted us with "Welcome to our Foreign Friends," smiling Chinese served green tea out of enormous flasks and offered us delicious little cakes. Playing cards, chess sets and dominoes were also offered.

We were clearly expected to make the best of our two-hour journey to the Wall. Listening to piped Mozart, we leaned back and watched the scenery through double-glazed, lace-curtained windows.

Flat fields dotted with peasants bent double at their tasks were followed by rising mountain slopes and stony screes.

The peasants were replaced by the occasional shepherd with his sheep. After a while even the shepherds disappeared, and we were left climbing ever upward, between great boulders that turned into crags, crags into peaks . . .

And then a great shout went up: "There it is!" And, yes, there it was, snaking upwards, a thin grey line with a ragged edge, and here and there a battlemented tower.

"You see," Mr Koo announced, smiling broadly. "Our Wall."

"That is where you climb," Mr Wong said.

After the comfort of the train, the mountainside looked very bare.

"Will it be very high?" I asked, a shade anxiously.

"Oh yes," Mr Koo said.

"And very cold?"

THERE'S A LONG, LONG WALL A-WINDING . . .

"Oh yes," Mr Wong said. "The winds blow from Mongolia."

I shuddered, and pulled my scarf closer round my head. Everest didn't seem so distant after all.

WE got off the train just beyond the Bridge of the Green Dragon, and plodded up a stony track along with all the other Westerners. We walked for quite half a mile on granite chips, and already my feet were killing me, though I hadn't even started to climb the Wall.

When at last we reached the cluster of grey buildings at the Wall's base, Mr Koo waved me courteously forward, as though saying, "After you." I took a deep breath and started to climb.

It wasn't too bad at first. I didn't dare look upwards, for the snaking stones went more and more steeply up towards the scudding clouds and the windy sky. But at least the paving beneath our feet was wide and smooth. Holding tight to my husband's arm, I peered over the edge.

Formidable ramparts plunged down the hillside. Our comfortable little train had gone away and wouldn't be back again till four o'clock.

It seemed a long time till four, with all of us human beings climbing the great mountainside like tiny flies upon a window-pane.

But Mr Koo and Mr Wong were encouraging. "Up, up!" they urged.

The ascent was rapidly getting steeper, the paving stones more craggy. When I took another peep over the edge, even the railway track seemed to have disappeared in rolling clouds of mist.

I told myself I was British, and remembered Mr Churchill and how the British never give in. With heart pumping and breath coming in gasps, I forced my buckling legs to stagger up the last gruelling stretch,

scrabbling at the balustrade with fingers and elbows to lever myself up — and suddenly, I was there.

Right at the top at last, and aching in every limb. But there was no denying it. I was Up the Wall.

Clinging to the stone coping on the topmost tower, I tried to imprint the scene on my memory. After all, I wouldn't be coming here again. From my position as King of the Castle, all I could see were mountains, more mountains and still more mountains.

Leaning over the parapet, I could just catch a glimpse of my husband, burdened with cameras, frantically signalling from his niche in the wall far below. I waved triumphantly, and if it hadn't been for all the others with me, I'd have let out a war-whoop as I charged downhill again.

"Going down!" I exulted, like some enthusiastic lift-attendant.

After the climb, the going was bliss. When I rejoined my husband and his cameras, we walked sedately down to report back to Mr Koo and Mr Wong, who had long since reached the bottom.

The little train did come at four o'clock, and we sat comfortably resting our aching legs on the cushioned seats, listening as improbably as ever to Mozart.

The green tea was going strong, the talk and laughter flowed, Mr Koo and Mr Wong were all one big beam of satisfaction, and so, at last, was I.

After all, it isn't every day that a housewife from Britain can climb so high that she can feel the wind from the Gobi Desert — or is it Mongolia? — fanning her cheek, and can shout: "I'm the King of the Castle" to the far-distant plains of Peking.

And if any of you astronauts happened to be looking from the Moon that day and noticed that little black speck waving from the Great Wall down to Earth — yes, you're right. That was me! □

A DAY OUT IN LONDON

Continued from page 11.

"I've always found it a dreadful bore myself," he said firmly. "I suppose it's all those tourists." He hailed a taxi, and heard Sally speaking quietly behind him.

"Goodbye, Mr Andrews. Thank you for putting up so well with two country bumpkins."

He whirled round. Her face was stricken, her eyes clouded with hurt.

"Sally —" he said quickly.

"Come on, Tommy." She grabbed the boy and ran for the approaching taxi. "Waterloo, please," she said crisply, bundling Tommy in and slamming the door.

They were gone.

Women! Couldn't she see he'd been enjoying himself? Didn't she realise he'd meant he'd always found London a bore — until today?

He could still feel the warmth of that small hand in his in The Chamber of Horrors; he remembered her eyes, her voice, the graceful walk. That girl had crept right into his heart.

"Taxi!" he yelled. "Waterloo — fast!"

After an agonising search of the destination boards he found the train to Nerston Edge. He raced along the platform, his eyes searching every window, until he found them.

The small, heart-shaped face was composed, yet sad. Tommy, catching sight of him, jumped up and let down the window.

"Hello, Mr Andrews," he said excitedly. "It's been a smashing day. Sally didn't give me a chance to say thanks."

"Hello, Tommy." Robert smiled at the boy, then tentatively stretched out a hand to touch Sally's.

"It's different with you," he said simply, and took her hand in his.

The cloud cleared from her eyes and they became warm. She understood.

"I need you with me, Sally. Without you, I feel . . . nothing. But everything is all right — with you by my side."

Doors banged along the train and whistles blew.

"Please — will you come back?" he asked.

"Yes." She nodded. "Of course I'll come. We'll go to Covent Garden next time."

He laughed and began to walk along the platform, still holding her hand, as the train began to draw out of the station.

"Where can I reach you . . . your address?"

Sally grinned. "If you ever find your briefcase again — you must have it in the file . . ."

The train gathered speed, and he dropped back. She blew him a kiss and he waved the train out of the station.

Robert turned and walked slowly away, picking up the briefcase from further down the platform.

He must remember to tell Miss Amery how very much he had enjoyed his day. □

From this day forward

It was the most wonderful, most unexpected gift ever — from the bride to her father.

THE front door slams. The last car sets off for the church, and we're alone, Debbie and I. Alone in a room — a house — that suddenly seems alien and over-large. A house that up until a few minutes ago was bustling with activity.

We look at each other in silence, my daughter and I. Then she smiles. "Would you like some coffee before we go, Dad?" she asks.

She doesn't say anything about calming my nerves, but I know it's what she's thinking all the same. I shake my head.

As Debbie picks up a cup for herself, I go over to her side.

"I'll do that," I offer quickly. "You don't want to spoil your dress, do you?"

"Yes." She laughs, and in that moment, to me, it's as if she's about seven years old again. "I can just imagine the report in the local rag — 'the bride wore white — patterned with polka dots of black coffee!' "

As she smooths the skirts of the lacy white gown my wife has taken so much time and trouble over, these past few hectic months, I feel a lump as big as an egg in my throat.

And I can hardly bear to look at her, because she is so beautiful. And so very vulnerable in that contraption that has had to become part of her young life.

"Are you all right, Debbie?" I am almost afraid to ask the question suddenly uppermost in my mind. I reach out, hesitantly, to touch her hand.

It would be unendurable — as much for me as for her — if my daughter had to bear pain today of all days. But she shakes her head, and squeezes my hand, a look I can't quite fathom in her beautiful eyes.

B

FROM THIS DAY FORWARD

As I carry her empty cup back to the table, I find myself thinking again of Debbie when she was little. How close we were in those days. How perfect everything had seemed.

"Just wait until you have to walk her down the aisle, and give her away!"

I remember Gwen's father saying that ruefully one day when Debbie, as usual, clambered on to my knee.

"That's a day neither of you will ever forget!"

My father-in-law couldn't have been more right about that, I think now, and the familiar agony rises inside me, blocking off all other emotions.

I am aware of Debbie watching me, as I walk to the window. I close my eyes, and my mind goes back, like a ghost, doomed to haunt the memory of that terrible day for ever.

IT had started off like any other day. Me rushing round getting ready for the office — Debbie taking up the bathroom. Gwen cooking breakfast, and generally organising both of us.

Then, just as she was leaving for her job at the local library, Debbie asked, "Will you run me over to Kev's tonight, Dad? We're going to a party, and the buses are so awkward after six."

Winking at Gwen, I'd pretended to grumble. "You and that fiancé of yours must think I'm a taxi service!"

"Have a heart, Dad!" Grinning, Debbie had dropped a kiss on my head as she passed my chair. "Surely you can just about remember what it was like when you and Mum were saving to get married all those years ago?"

"Cheeky young madam!" I called, as she breezed out of the house, and Gwen and I looked at each other across her empty chair, and exchanged a smile.

Neither of us knew then it was to be the last smile we were going to share for a long time.

It was an ordinary day. An ordinary evening, until, on my way to Debbie's fiancé's house, I hit that patch of black ice on the road, and skidded . . .

After that, the nightmare really began. The sickening horror of being told that, though my cuts and bruises were superficial, my daughter had been more seriously injured.

"Debbie was in the passenger side of the car that actually hit the brick wall." The doctor's words are written indelibly on my brain.

"Though the damage to her spine may not be irrevocable, she will, for the time being, at any rate, have to be confined to a wheelchair."

"The car's here, Dad."

She reaches out her hand to me. As I take it, I think of the times since the accident that I've been told it wasn't my fault. That I mustn't keep punishing myself the way I do.

But I am only too aware that if it weren't for my carelessness, Debbie would be walking out to the waiting limousine with me now.

The driver says nothing, as I fold the chair, and lift it carefully inside the car, but I can feel his sympathy for this beautiful bride with the strangely-determined little face.

Anxiety rises inside me again as I think of all the problems ahead of her and Kevin.

I REMEMBER how, after the accident, both Gwen and I begged Debbie to wait.

"The date is set, Dad," Debbie had said firmly. "Kev and I love each other — and we don't see any reason to wait, just because I'm like this."

"I'll look after her, Mr Mitchell." Kevin's young, earnest voice drifts back to me, as I sit beside Debbie in the wedding taxi. "You've no need to worry about that!"

But no matter how he cossets Debbie in the future, nothing will alter what I, her own father, have done to her . . .

Quite suddenly, it seems, we are at the church, the church where Gwen and I made our vows, nearly twenty years ago.

I open the taxi door, and lift Debbie out, while the driver, thoughtfully, helps with the chair. They will all be waiting, family and friends.

And Gwen, especially Gwen, looking younger than ever, in her new, pale-blue dress, with only the shadows in her eyes to betray her pain.

The limousine disappears, and once again Debbie and I are alone. Trying not to think of how things might have been, I push Debbie slowly up to the church door.

We are right by the door when Debbie suddenly says, quite quietly, but with a firmness I've never heard before — "Stop!"

Next moment, she is half-turning in the chair — raising up her two arms to me, as she used to when she was small.

"Help me up, Dad," she says, as I stare, unable to believe my ears.

"But . . .?" Even as I begin to protest, Debbie is pulling herself up by my side.

"You — you can't go in without the chair, love," I whisper, as thick tears block my throat. "You can't . . ."

Debbie turns her head and looks at me with her clear, sparkling eyes. Her mother's eyes that have seen so much that hasn't been good, these past few months.

"I can Dad!" she whispers, as my heart nearly leaps right out of me. "I've been practising. I haven't even told Kev, let alone Mum, but I can manage quite a few steps now. I wanted to walk down the aisle, for — for you, and for me . . ."

"You'll give her away," my father-in-law had said. But as the organ strikes up the familiar tune, and we make our first, slow steps into that church full of astonishment and wonder, I know I could never give my daughter away.

Because of this moment that gives us both back our future, she will remain in my proud heart for ever . . . □

Complete Story By **ISOBEL STEWART**

That's No Lady

When a wife feels her husband doesn't appreciate her, sometimes all she has to do is strike a spark of jealousy!

I T'S asking for trouble, Margy," my husband said darkly.
I looked up from trying to find the missing partners for three of
his socks, and asked him what was asking for trouble.

"All these business trips. All this leaving you alone so much. It's
asking for trouble," Jeff said again, even more darkly.

I sat back on my heels, and looked at him, surprised, but
delighted. I mean, it's not every man who thinks his wife is a *femme*

fatale after 10 years of marriage. Maybe he thought Robert Redford was waiting to woo me as soon as he left.

But I didn't say that.

Instead, I said lovingly: "You don't have to worry, Jeff. You can trust me."

"I know you'll try," he went on. "But when I was away last, you paid the chemist twice, you missed paying the credit cards, you scraped the car, and you tried to clear the drains yourself, and made them worse. So you must admit I'm right — it's asking for trouble, leaving you alone."

I felt like a deflated balloon. He wasn't worried about me running off with Robert Redford, he was only worried about the bills and the car and the drains.

I stood up. "I made a mistake with the bills," I admitted coolly, "but I'll be more careful this time. And the car was your own fault, you left the wheelbarrow sticking out in the garage. If there's any problem with the drains, which there will be, I'll call the plumber, OK?"

I don't think he even noticed the ice dripping from my voice.

"Do that," he agreed. "Margy, where are the pairs for these socks?"

"Lost," I told him briefly and unsympathetically. "I suspect your daughter put them down the toilet, and I bet that didn't do the drains any good either!"

This time he got the message.

"Are you annoyed with me?" he enquired, surprised.

I tried to give one of those light, tinkling laughs, but it didn't quite come off. To tell the truth, it sounded something like the drain does when it's blocked. Which it always is, because Jeff wanted an old house with atmosphere. Atmosphere it has, but it also has drains.

He's a practical man, my husband — he has to be — so when I said I wasn't angry with him he accepted that with relief, and went on to give me concise and brisk intructions about the bills that I'd have to pay while he was away. And before leaving, he gave me a full-bodied kiss that left me kind of breathless.

But once I'd got my breath back and strapped Suzie into her car seat, and told her we were going to meet Robbie at school, I began to do some thinking again. By the time we'd picked up Robbie, I knew that there was something far wrong with my image if the only thing Jeff couldn't trust me with was the drains. And the bills and car.

Don't get me wrong. I love my husband dearly, but what I wanted to know was this: what had happened to the fellow who used to scowl with jealousy when his colleagues danced with me at office parties? The fellow who used to ask me what exactly old so-and-so said, and why he had to hold me so close?

And, perhaps even more important, what had happened to the girl that made him feel as if all the males in the world were just waiting their chance to grab her away from him?

That night, when the children were in bed. I took a long, critical look at myself in the bedroom mirror. Had I let myself go? And if I had, could I get myself back?

I hadn't really put on weight, in spite of having had two children. Running after them gave me all the exercise I needed!

My hair was straighter than it used to be, partly for easiness, but mostly because I liked it better that way. Maybe I did dress differently now, but then my life-style was different. Casual, I would call it.

And I'd tried to stay interesting, too. All right, until Suzie went to nursery school I'd had to lay aside the degree course in English I was doing, but maybe next year I'd get back to it. The degree course was planned, you see, and Suzie wasn't, but we'd rather have her than any degree.

I looked at myself again.

The next day I had my hair done, and I skipped lunch. While Suzie had her nap I got out *Comedy Of Errors* and read it. And I took a skirt from my wardrobe and wore it instead of my slacks.

Robbie said my hair was nice, and my skirt was too short. Suzie looked at me as if she wasn't too sure we'd been introduced, and then she grabbed my leg and laddered my stocking.

THE next day, the drains went.

Jeff has a long wire that he used to unclog them. It's like being a lion-tamer, the drains know his touch right away, and they behave beautifully. They clear themselves with an apologetic sort of gurgle, as if they hadn't really meant to cause all this trouble. They also know when it's me on the other end of the wire, and they block themselves up even more.

So I did as I'd promised, and called the plumber.

Now, I don't know how plumbers come. in your neighbourhood, but I'd never had a plumber like this one. Jeff is so practical that we really don't need a plumber very often, but I had this picture of a small stout man with glasses and an air of brisk efficiency about him.

The one who came had the air of efficiency, but he was tall and dark, and really, he looked more like a film star than a plumber.

But he was no film star, he got the measure of our drains right away. They gave in just as they do for Jeff.

I was so grateful I asked him if he'd like a cup of coffee. He accepted politely, and we sat down at the kitchen table, chaperoned by Suzie and the dog.

We had a lovely chat about the merits of old houses with atmosphere and drains, against new houses with no atmosphere and no plumbing problems.

"Oh, Mummy," Suzie interrupted, reproachfully, looking with surprise at the little pool around her feet.

"Oh, Suzie," I said, and took her off to change her into dry pants.

When I came back, the dog and Mr Johnson, the plumber, had been making each other's acquaintance, and he said he hoped I didn't mind if he helped himself to more coffee.

He told me he had a little girl about Suzie's age, and we talked about potty-training, and then he asked if I knew anything about croup, because they'd had such a fright the other night when their three-month-old baby had had it. So we talked about croup, and we discussed feeding problems, and

when we went down the garden path he admired my geranium and I gave him a clipping from it, and he promised to give me a little fuchsia plant.

I really felt I knew him well by the time he left, and I assured him that I'd call him again if the drains misbehaved.

But the drains behaved perfectly all the rest of the time Jeff was away.

The day he was due back, I had my hair done again, and I wore my skirt — the length Robbie said it should be — and I saw that Suzie didn't get near enough to ladder my stockings.

When we met Jeff at the airport it took him a little while to get around to noticing me, what with Robbie and the baby throwing themselves at him. But when he did, I felt it was worth all the effort.

He raised his eyebrows.

"Who is this lady?" he asked Robbie.

He knew what he had to say, and he said it.

"That's no lady, that's Mummy!" he told him laughing.

Jeff raised his eyebrows again, and clapped his hand to his forehead. "Good heavens, I do believe you're right," he said.

By then everyone was staring at us, and Suzie was jumping up and down with excitement and maybe something else. I took her off to the cloakroom and then we went home.

After Jeff had unpacked, I poured him a drink, and I poured one for myself. I told Robbie he could bath Suzie, although I knew the bathroom would look like a disaster area when they'd finished. Then I sat down opposite Jeff and sipped my drink.

But he kept looking at me in much the same way Suzie had. When our eyes met, he said quickly and unconvincingly, "I like your hair that way, Margy, it's — different, isn't it?"

I put my drink down. "You don't really like it, do you?"

"I prefer it the other way," he said honestly. And then, a little desperately: "You look very nice, but you look like a visitor."

He came over beside me then, and took me on his knee. A little while later I looked much too rumpled to be a visitor.

Then our two-year-old streaker came running downstairs, dripping, and Jeff chased her and took her back upstairs to dry her. I'd just gone through to the kitchen, when I heard the doorbell ring.

It was the plumber.

"I've brought you a fuchsia plant," he said. "I was passing this way."

He told me exactly what to do about planting it, so that it would settle nicely, and then I asked about his baby's croup, and when we'd talked about that we moved just outside the door so that I could show him where I was going to plant the fuchsia. Then the dog saw him and did his stupid act of rolling over on his back with his feathery paws in the air, and the plumber tickled his tummy for him and the dog rolled over some more.

I SAID goodbye, and when I turned round from waving to him, there was Jeff standing at the door, looking somehow as if he'd been there for some time.

"Who was that?" he asked.

"The plumber," I told him.

"The plumber?" he repeated, astonished. Then he looked at the fuchsia plant in my hand.

"He brought me this," I explained unnecessarily.

"I didn't hear the dog bark at him," Jeff said, ignoring the fuchsia.

"Well, you see, he was here for quite a while the other day, when he came to see the drains, and the dog made friends with him."

For absolutely no reason in the world, I blushed.

"We were talking about his baby having croup," I said. Although it was the absolute truth, I knew as I said it that it sounded completely unconvincing, and I blushed again.

"He — he has a little girl the same age as Suzie," I added, and somehow that didn't sound any more truthful.

Jeff looked at me thoughtfully.

"I was saving this to tell you later," he said. "But I think I'll tell you right now. I've been offered a job at head office. It means a bigger salary, and it means an end to travelling away from home. I hate the idea of leaving this house, but I spent an afternoon looking around, and I think we should find something we like fairly easily."

"An old house with atmosphere, of course," I suggested, and I could feel laughter bubbling inside me.

"Of course," Jeff agreed suspiciously. And then, with sudden doubt, he looked down at me. "You do want another house something like this one, Margy?"

"Of course I do," I said, meaning it. "I love this house. Drains and all."

He closed the front door behind us, and took me in his arms and kissed me soundly.

When he let me go, I looked up and saw the children on the landing, watching us with interest.

"You've untidied Mummy's hair," Robbie said.

"So I have," Jeff agreed, with satisfaction. "So I have."

And he kissed me once again, just to make certain. □

She was just a little Cocker spaniel, but she was to become my constant companion, continual source of amusement and a great comfort on our many walks through life . . .

By GIDEON SCOTT MAY

This MAN and his DOG

FROM time to time I have been sentenced to a period in the "dog house" by my wife, Irralee, or our daughter, Shona or both.

Then one day they pooled their resources to keep me out of mischief by presenting me with a pedigree Cocker spaniel puppy.

The puppy had been carefully chosen. It had character with a capital "C." One eye slumbered deeply in the centre of a black patch whilst the other, with its white surround, gave an honest, direct look at everyone and everything. The rest of her body was dotted with dark spots that shaded themselves, one by one, into a white background, finishing with a carefree black splash over her rear complete with a little black tail with a white tip that was the next thing to perpetual motion.

"What," the petticoats asked in unison, "are you going to call her?"

Without a moment's hesitation, I said, "That's Ceilidh. I can tell by her wriggly, squiggly, fun-loving approach and the little, pink tongue that's laughing at life."

Next day, I took Ceilidh with me on a tree-felling expedition. I carried her under my arm whenever the little legs looked like getting tired, and we covered a good half-mile before reaching the chosen tree.

As I opened up the base of the tree with an axe, the pup played with the chips as they flew around. Then I got down to the serious business with a bushman's saw. I judged the tree would fall just along the inside of the fence. Ceilidh was lying just behind me.

GIDEON'S WAY

More impressions of life from the Highlands of Scotland, by Gideon Scott May, observer of people and nature alike . . .

I turned my attention to the saw. It did its work. I shouted "Tim-ber," the recognised warning to all who may find themselves in the path of a falling tree.

Then I looked round to find Ceilidh. She was no longer there! I made a quick circle round, then a wider one. There was no sign of her. What, I thought anxiously, if she had strayed on to the road? I leaped the fence and gazed up and down, but there was nothing.

Could she have reached the lochside? I raced down to the water's edge. I could see a considerable distance each way, but there was nothing there either.

26

Doubling back through the wood, but again finding nothing, I listened for the sound of a lost puppy's whimper, but the only sound I heard was a tap-tap-tapping from a blue-tit busy boring a hole in a hazelnut.

It took all the courage I could muster to go back to Irralee and Shona and confess that I had lost my puppy on our very first outing together. As I opened the door nervously, there was Ceilidh, lying flat on her back, in front of the fire. Her eyes were closed blissfully as Irralee tickled her tubby, little tummy.

She had found her way home, travelling over half a mile all on her own. At an early age, she had proved her independence.

MY feelings for Ceilidh were soon to be tested to the limit when, after a hot and exhausting afternoon, she and I set off for a swim.

Together, we slipped into the water. Ceilidh swam beside me with her refined dog-paddle.

As I dried myself with my kilt, Ceilidh suddenly gave a short, sharp bark. She never speaks unless it is something really important. It was! She was face to face with an adder, raised on its tail almost to the level of her nose and poised ready to strike.

Old Cranna, a gamekeeper, had shown me how to pick up an adder, by placing the thumb and forefinger behind its head with the speed of lightning. It had to be distracted, then you seized it quickly by the tail and cracked the snake like a whip.

"It's something you do," he said, "only once."

The snake confronting Ceilidh was a big, green and black male.

I matched the hiss of the snake. "Sit."

Ceilidh obliged, almost in slow motion, never taking her eyes off her adversary. Creeping, like an Indian, around the rocks, I found the tip of the snake's tail. Seizing it between my thumb and forefinger, and in one lightning movement, I swung the adder in a full circle and banged its head on a big boulder. The snake writhed for a moment then lay still.

I stood there in the heat of the sun with my teeth chattering.

Ceilidh still sat obediently, with a look of sheer astonishment on the white half of her face. Dropping to my knees, I flung my arms around her neck. Ceilidh seemed to sense that I was trembling and her warm, velvety muzzle whispered soft, soothing, reassuring sounds in my ear.

It was in that moment that I realised the growing strength of the bond between us, and the measure of my love for this little, spotted spaniel. □

A Lifetime of Loving

Complete Story By
JANET HARTSHORNE

The tiny bundle of mischief grew into a tired old lady — but she gave her family everything she had to give . . .

NEVER again! I vow silently as I wave my family off for the day, forcing a smile to my frozen lips.

"See you tonight, Mummy!" Such a sad little effort on the part of my youngest daughter to appear normal, to prove that she is all right. When my whole being aches for her and for the pain which wasn't there yesterday — which wasn't there less than two hours ago when I stood looking down at her and her sleeping sister, postponing the awful moment when I must shatter warm childish dreams with cold reality.

"She was very old," I told them, amongst other hopelessly-inadequate words. "How many other dogs have lived for nearly sixteen years?" And bravely they agreed — we'd been lucky . . . very lucky.

It had to happen sooner or later, I told myself as I plaited hair and packed lunches, and made a breakfast that no-one really wanted. And all the time, every muscle in my face ached and I vowed that never, ever, would there be a next time. Never again would there be another Patsy.

Now they've gone, and I don't have to pretend any more.

Gazing out across a blur of garden, I don't have to fake consolation in the fact that she was old, or try to convince myself that being prepared has made it any easier. It hasn't made it easier at all.

Can it really be fifteen years since that black mongrel pup was offered to a good home? It seems like yesterday. And yet, doesn't "for ever" span that tiny, tottering bundle of mischief and the tired old lady

29

who preferred to doze her days away under the kitchen table?

Funny, but we never intended having a dog. Dogs were a tie then, I remember, the years rolling away. It was a sudden fascination for everything on four legs by our exuberant two-year-old which sent her devoted father dashing out to collect one cast-off pup.

We were blissfully unaware of what lay in store.

"Try an alarm clock tucked beneath her blanket!" a friend advised after two sleepless nights.

"A hot-water bottle . . . cuddly toys . . .!" others suggested.

Only a desperate man slumped uncomfortably across the sitting-room couch, one hand hanging limply in her basket, eventually quietened our noisily-pining pup.

At first, she couldn't, or wouldn't, walk. She only dropped her hangdog expression, perfected over years, when squashed into the push-chair beside her beloved companion.

But gradually the thought of dragging her owners bodily along became more attractive than riding. It took a while before the fact that dogs slept in baskets and humans in beds was finally accepted.

I stand, hands immersed in suds, not washing up yet, just letting the comforting warmth creep into my arms. And I recall the speculation of those early days — the endless guessing as to what breed Patsy would eventually resemble.

"What sort *is* it, exactly?" people would ask in passing, eyeing the big paws, pointed nose and flapping ears in barely-concealed disbelief.

"We think she could maybe have some Alsatian in her . . . or terrier," we'd tell them hopefully. "Or corgi?"

"With those paws!" They'd laugh. "Never!" And then we would ask ourselves why . . . why hadn't we gone in for some definite, clear-cut variety of animal?

But Patsy refused to aim anything but high.

Enough's enough, we insisted firmly, once she and the handsome golden Labrador from down the road had produced their second litter of Labradorable pups.

"That fence has got to be fixed!" I declared frantically as two dozen tiny legs scampered around the family's feet.

I DRY my hands and make my way down the garden to scatter the leftover crusts for the birds and, all the time, I try not to miss the padding paws which invariably used to follow.

For a moment, I stand soaking up the sunshine. How did one dog manage to create more trouble for me than three, normal, mischievous youngsters?

"I'll have that blasted hound put down, so help me!" our neighbour would warn us repeatedly, brandishing some mutilated piece of foliage over the fence. "She wants chaining up!"

"Never again!" I'd warn the children, dragging a repentant animal back to the house. "Never will I have another dog as long as I live!"

Slowly, incident by incident, memory by memory, the days unfold for me. My babies became children, children young adults — with too much happening in their overflowing lives to miss a childhood companion for too long. Which is as it should be.

But me . . . how long will I miss you, old dog, I wonder.

How long before I learn to live without, or forget, the feel of a cold nose nuzzled into my palm . . . the trust in velvet eyes . . . the unfailing, ecstatic welcome after even the briefest separation?

How do you say goodbye to a dog, I ask myself now. What small tribute says thank you — thank you for a lifetime of friendship?

A photograph — framed and placed amongst the books and mementoes, the ornaments and school photographs which line the sitting-room shelves? I think not. It would simply say "once we had a dog" — nothing more.

The fence needs fixing again, I notice, but there is none of the urgency of those earlier, destructive days.

Don't some people mark the spot where a beloved pet lies? I remember the various home-made headstones which depicted the graves of ill-fated birds and hamsters, when our three were small . . . the tiny jars filled with daisies by loving fingers.

Today, there is a patch of newly-turned earth beneath the apple tree — partially covered even now by dry leaves and twigs in a deliberate effort to conceal, to leave no reminder.

Strange that no-one, this morning, asked where, or when, or how. It was as though they too could only bear to remember her living — the warm, affectionate, boundless living which has no part in a framed photograph or patch of marked earth.

And, suddenly, I'm sure. There is only one way to remember, to fill the empty gap her going has left.

★   ★   ★   ★

I go into the house, towards the phone.

I'm a fool, I tell myself as I search for the number I need.

There'll be sleepless nights, and possessions chewed to ribbons. There'll be irate neighbours and more than one enraged tradesman. And there'll be the tie, the encumbrance, the inconvenience.

And then, somewhere in the distant future, there'll be the pain And I will vow, a dozen times, "Never again!"

But there'll be so much more, too. There'll be loving in abundance, and the kind of loyalty few friends can offer.

And, once more, the place will feel right — it will be home again.

Well-meaning friends will frown indulgently as they survey our newest member of the family.

"What sort is it?" they'll undoubtedly ask, wondering why we should take on yet another all-sorts dog, a dog with no class, who leaves endless doubts about its ancestors. And maybe we'll wonder, too. But not for long.

No words can say as much as the scraggy cast-off we will, in all probability, inherit.

Nothing else pays better tribute to someone well loved, than saying, "That was great! Let's do it again!" □

Those That Help Themselves

Blessed was the Reverend Josiah Meeke, despite inheriting a crumbling old church. For he was just wicked enough to do something about it.

GOOD morning, Mr Taylor. 'Morning, Walter. Hello, Mrs Prescott, nice to see you."

The Reverend Josiah Meeke adjusted thick-rimmed spectacles and beamed with myopic geniality as his flock slowly filtered out of the church.

"What a beautiful sermon for Centenary Week. So appropriate!" Old Miss Engleton gushed as he shook her hand. "But it's such a pity it's your last. We'll all be so sorry to lose you."

"Oh, I think you'll be quite safe in Mr Miller's hands," he assured her, indicating the young man at his side. "And I trust you'll give him as much support as you gave me.

"Good morning, Mrs Blythe." He shook the next hand in line. "You'll remember the Guild are serving tea in the church hall this morning, won't you?"

As the last member of his congregation filed out, Josiah turned to the Reverend Mr Miller.

"Well, Brian, it's all yours now," he said, patting the younger man's shoulder. "I hope you'll have as many happy years in St Mary's as I've had."

Together they walked over to the vicarage.

"You must be sorry to go," Brian said. "After all the years you've spent here, it must be quite a wrench."

Josiah thought about it, then shook his head.

"No, I don't think I will," he said slowly. "I'd like to think I've earned my retirement. I'll be quite happy to potter about in the garden, and listen to you doing the work on a Sunday morning!

"And anyway, I've seen the quatercentenary year. 1579 to 1979, St

c

Mary's has stood. It was always my dream to see her into her fifth century, and with God's help, I've done that.

"Time now for some young blood to take over."

Brian stopped in the hall and smiled nervously.

"You know, you're quite a man to live up to, Josiah. You've worked so hard for the church, and for the village. No matter how hard I try, I know I can never be even half the person you are."

"Nonsense!" Josiah declared.

He was silent for a moment, frowning, and then made up his mind.

"To tell the truth, Brian," he said solemnly, "I'm really a very wicked man.

"Yes, wicked," Josiah repeated as the younger man raised an incredulous eyebrow. "No-one else knows the story, but I think now I'd like to get it off my chest.

"You see, it all began one Tuesday morning about — oh, almost three years ago now . . . "

★　　　★　　　★　　　★

That Tuesday morning had seemed perfectly ordinary when Josiah got up, after yet another sleepless night.

"You should have had a long lie, dear," his wife said fussily as he started on his boiled egg. "I know the pain must keep you from sleeping, but you really can't go on without any rest."

Josiah looked down at his left foot, recently out of plaster and now supported by a thick crêpe bandage. It was still rather painful, he had to admit, but then as Doctor Forbes had pointed out, it was his own silly fault. Any man of 63 who went about climbing ladders deserved to fall off.

And he had been very lucky, to get off with a broken ankle. He thanked the good Lord for that.

It was just a pity, Josiah couldn't help thinking, that He in His infinite wisdom hadn't seen fit for Josiah to fall *after* he'd plastered over the crack in the wall of the church, not *before*.

As it was, the crack was still there, growing bigger every day, just as his foot had done.

Josiah shook his head wearily. Anyway, Winifred was wrong in thinking the pain was the cause of his sleepless nights. Pain can — indeed, should — be borne bravely. In time it would go away.

Unfortunately, the problem at the root of his insomnia wouldn't go away so easily.

Finishing his breakfast, Josiah hobbled round to the church.

Thirty-seven preachers had stood in that pulpit before him, Josiah thought as he looked up at the old, beautifully-carved stone building. At one time he had been able to reel off the list of names, but his memory wasn't quite what it had been.

His short-sighted gaze swept over the church, taking in the crumbling plaster, the damp patches where the roof leaked. The two-foot crack that had widened alarmingly over the lancet window on the east wall.

What would the 37 have said if they could see the place now? Somehow, it seemed a betrayal of them that he should be the one to let it all go.

He sighed. Money, that was the problem; or rather, the lack of it. The powers that be had already spent so much on the upkeep of St Mary's Church, and it had been made quite clear that no more would be forthcoming.

They were right in their way, Josiah supposed. It did seem a waste to go on pouring limited resources into an old building with no real architectural merit. Especially when the small congregation could quite easily be accommodated in the new parish church over in Dunswick.

Not that it would be the same, of course. Old and failing though the church might be, it was their own, and the congregation loved it. They had proved that by their efforts to raise money for the repairs.

Seven thousand pounds, Josiah thought. Even the hardest-working congregation couldn't hope to raise a sum like that by jumble sales and church fêtes — especially in the short time they had before the axe fell. Or the roof, which ever came first.

Leaning heavily on his stick, Josiah returned to the vicarage, and buttoned himself into his overcoat. He would have one last try with the bishop, and if that failed . . .

Well, no doubt the congregation would soon settle down quite happily in Dunswick Parish.

And as for himself, Josiah thought as he got off the town bus and made his way down Main Street — well, it was about time he retired anyway. He had wanted so much to hang on until the quatercentenary year. But if the church went, so would his dream.

He was getting past it now; had fulfilled his usefulness to God and the community. It was high time he accepted that, and stopped bumbling on like a silly old man.

He turned the corner into the square, and was just passing the bank when a man came out and collided with him.

Knocked off balance, Josiah gripped his sleeve in an effort to save himself.

"Oh dear, I'm so sorry." He started to apologise, and then his bad ankle gave way under him, suddenly and painfully.

Thrusting out his cane, Josiah was vaguely aware of it connecting with a second person before he toppled over, dragging the two down with him.

The sound of a woman screaming was the last thing he heard as his head struck the pavement.

JOSIAH wasn't quite sure where he was when he came round. Looking up at a white ceiling, he struggled to raise himself, and was gently pushed back on to pillows.

"Just lie still, Mr Meeke," a soft but authoritative voice instructed. "The doctor will be here in a moment."

Obeying the voice, Josiah lay still. He didn't really feel much like

35

moving anyway, not even when the white-coated man came in to poke and prod at him, and finally, with a genial smile, pronounced him none the worse for his exploits.

"There you are! Just a few days' rest and you'll be as right as rain," the nurse said after the doctor had departed. "We were beginning to get quite worried about you. You've been unconscious for nearly twenty-four hours."

Josiah blinked in surprise.

"But — what happened?" he asked vaguely.

"These should jog your memory."

The nurse moved to a table on the other side of the small private room, and returned with a bundle of newspapers.

"Last night's and this morning's, " she said brightly. "I've been saving them for you. It's not often we get a hero in the hospital."

"A hero?" Josiah frowned in perplexity, and picked up the newspaper on top of the bundle.

He stared open-mouthed at the headline.

"VICAR FOILS MASKED RAIDERS!" it announced boldly.

"MEEKE — BUT NOT MILD!" the second quipped.

With a sinking feeling in his stomach, Josiah read on. He discovered how the Reverend J. P. Meeke had single-handedly attacked two armed men making their getaway from the main branch of the town bank with the best part of £1,000,000 in used bank notes.

He looked up from the small print and stared dazedly at the nurse.

"Fancy tackling them like that!" she said admiringly. "And you a man of the cloth, too!"

"But — but I really didn't do anything at all!" Josiah protested.

Memory was coming back, slowly but surely. The bank. Two men coming out. He'd bumped into one of them, hadn't he? Not looking where he was going, probably. Winifred always got on to him for that.

And then he'd reached out with his stick, and —

"Now don't be modest," the nurse was saying. "There was a girl across the road, and she saw the whole thing. She said you just grabbed one of them by the arm, and bashed the other over the head with a cane."

"But really," Josiah said wildly, his distress growing greater by the minute, "I didn't — "

"Sssh, now," she said firmly. "You've done enough talking for the moment. The police will want to take a statement from you, but that can wait.

"You can see your wife, now — and Sir John too, if you promise to keep quiet and just listen."

Josiah was about to ask who Sir John might be, but Winifred was in the room before he got the chance, with a tall man behind her.

"You silly, brave man!" Winifred declared as she bent to kiss him. "It was a foolhardy thing to do, but — oh, I'm so proud of you!"

Josiah gulped.

Continued on page 38.

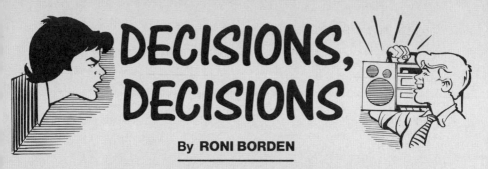

DECISIONS, DECISIONS

By RONI BORDEN

Why is it that in every family the voice of authority rarely seems to belong to poor old Mum?

MY children have a high regard for the voice of authority. Unfortunately, the voice doesn't happen to come from my lips. Their voice of authority can come from the mouths of (1) their friends, (2) the people who write for teenage magazines, (3) disc jockeys, and (4) their teachers.

"You'd better get all that clutter picked up from the floor of your room tonight," I say.

"But my social studies teacher said we have to hand in a five-page outline on the events leading up to the French Revolution."

How can I argue?

While I try to tolerate the musical preferences of other members of the household, a sense of survival forces me to fight back.

"Turn that radio down," I scream.

"But my favourite disc jockey says that you can only appreciate this music if it comes through at the proper volume!"

And so it goes!

But I finally decided that the time had come to re-establish my authority.

"Hi," I said to them when they got home from school. "Had a good day? What are you going to do this afternoon?"

Each one had a different appointment with various friends.

"Maybe you should start your homework first," I suggested.

"Oh, homework won't take more than half an hour, Mum. We have plenty of time."

Come evening, I assigned them tasks.

"You will set the table," I said, pointing to my son. "And the girls will do the washing up."

"But, Mum," they groaned, "my teacher . . ."

"Your teacher gave you homework that will take only half an hour to complete," I said cheerfully, and walked away.

Teenage magazines, however, are far more difficult to overcome.

"It says here," my daughter said one evening, looking up from her magazine, "if I put eggs beaten on my face for half an hour a day, my skin will become beautiful."

"Isn't that odd," I said. "I just clipped an article from the newspaper that says that the best thing to keep skin looking beautiful is plenty of hot water and soap."

Still, I have solved most of these problems.

"From now on, you can only listen to the radio while you clean your rooms or wash the dishes."

The children are more tidy now, still popular with their friends, and only keep the radio on for a reasonable amount of time.

And, fortunately, I have just discovered the one thing that establishes me as the final and supreme authority in the house. I hand out the pocket money! □

THOSE THAT HELP THEMSELVES

Continued from page 36.

"This is Sir John," she went on, "the chairman of the bank. He's been waiting nearly four hours to see you!"

"And I would have waited another four," Sir John said, reaching out to shake his hand. "It's an honour and a privilege to meet you, and to offer my personal thanks."

Josiah listened in deepening perplexity as he went on. What a fine upstanding citizen — such courage — if only there were more like him — be a reward, of course.

"Reward!" Josiah squeaked in horror. "Oh, but I couldn't possibly. If you'll just let me explain — "

"It always encourages the public to have a go when they see courage suitably rewarded." Sir John swept on relentlessly, taking not the slightest notice. "Taking into account our usual percentage in these cases, we thought something in the region of eight thousand would be an appropriate token of our gratitude."

"Please! Will you listen to me?" Josiah began desperately, then stopped short. "*How* much did you say?"

"Eight thousand," Sir John repeated casually. "Sorry, you were trying to tell me something?"

Josiah sank down under the bedclothes.

"Just that I was feeling a bit tired," he said in a small voice. "Would you mind very much if I have a rest now?"

They went away, and left him to think.

Eight thousand, Josiah thought. *Pounds*!

Of course, he would have to tell everyone what really happened, and there would be no question of giving him such a sum of money. It was meant as a reward for outstanding bravery, for fearlessly tackling two dangerous men, without thought to his personal safety.

He hadn't done that, so he had no right to a reward.

But just think of it, a voice purred in his ear. *Eight thousand pounds: enough to fix the roof on the church, and to do all the structural repairs.*

And perhaps even some left over to install central heating. Maybe even enough for stained-glass windows!

Josiah sat back on his pillows and sighed dreamily. Stained-glass windows! He had always wanted stained-glass windows.

But of course there was no use thinking about it. Better to confess right away, and put the whole idea out of his head.

But why, the voice persisted. *After all, you've already tried to explain and they wouldn't listen.*

Josiah tutted, shocked at himself. Of course he would have to tell them. It would be dishonest not to. It would be taking money under false pretences.

On the other hand, though, would it really? So much good could come of that money — not just for him and the church, but for the whole community.

And after all, he might have tackled the men, mightn't he? Accident or design, the outcome was the same as far as the bank was concerned . . .

"All right if I have a word with you now, sir?" a young policeman asked, popping his head round the door. "It won't take long. I think we know most of it already."

"Oh, I do hope so," Josiah said fearfully. "I'm afraid it's all a bit vague to me."

"The bump on the head, you know," he added apologetically.

"Quite understandable, sir," the policeman said. "Now, according to reports from other witnesses, I gather things must have happened something like this."

Josiah listened, still struggling with himself, as the policeman read off his view of events.

"That about right, sir?" he finished.

Josiah raised his eyes heavenwards and crossed his fingers.

"Yes, I suppose you could say that's what happened."

The thunderbolt that he was half-expecting failed to materialise.

★   ★   ★   ★

Josiah looked up from the floor into the eyes of St Mary's new vicar.

"So you see," he finished lamely, "I'm just a wicked old fraud."

"Do you think — " he hesitated — "do you think it was really *very* bad of me?"

Brian Miller regarded him straight-faced for a moment.

"Do you?" he asked.

Josiah gave a mischievous, half-hearted chuckle.

"I did at first," he admitted. "I used to worry about it all the time.

"But then after a while, when I saw the roof stop leaking, and the walls being strengthened, and the whole church coming to life again — well, they do say that the end can sometimes justify the means, don't they?"

He raised a shaggy eyebrow hopefully.

Brian laughed.

"And I'd say that this is one of the items when they certainly did."

He broke off as Winifred Meeke came into the room, and Josiah got to his feet.

"There you are!" she said accusingly. 'We've been waiting for you in the hall. The Guild has a presentation to make."

"Coming, dear," Josiah said, taking her arm. "Brian and I have just been talking about — about — "

" — about how God sometimes moves in mysterious ways, his wonders to perform," Brian Miller finished unctuously.

"Quite," the Reverend Josiah Meeke agreed, with an innocent smile. □

ROVER'S RETURN

He was a scruffy, disobedient, delinquent — but smarter than the average owner!

R IGHT, that's it!" I announced angrily as I dripped into the living-room. "A week now I've got soaked to the skin. That scruffy, ungrateful dog can jolly well stay lost for all I care!"

My mother laid aside her embroidery and regarded me dolefully. "No luck, Ian?"

"No," I replied patiently, though the dogless leash clutched in my frost-bitten hand spoke for itself.

Whatever other deficiencies Rover might have, he certainly wasn't lacking in the brains department. Which is more than can be said for me. I'd been soft hearted enough to take pity on him when he appeared at the door a month ago, half starved and shivering.

Honestly, that was gratitude for you! You take in a stray dog, feed it, walk it, worm it, provide it with every creature comfort and what does it do?

Runs off the minute your back is turned, that's what!

"Well, if he thinks I'm going to spend another night trailing about town shouting 'Rover' every two minutes, he's got another think coming," I said firmly. "I've had enough."

"Quite right, Ian," my mother declared, returning her attention to her embroidery.

"I mean, it's not as if I owe him anything, is it?" I persisted. "If a dog can't recognise a good home when he sees one, it's hardly my fault. I don't see why I should risk pneumonia just to fetch him back."

She didn't reply, and I brooded silently for a moment, letting the warmth of the fire blot out memories of a cold winter's night.

"On the other hand, of course, maybe he's been hurt," I went on eventually.

"It's not very likely though. The mutt's indestructible. He's got that sly cunning that'll let him survive anything."

"Yes, I expect you're quite right." Mother smiled placidly.

"But on the *other* hand, if he *was* hurt — "

"I'll have one last try. Perhaps the dog-catchers have got him. I'll go over to the home first thing tomorrow."

I mean, what else could I do? I wasn't worried myself but I could see my poor old mum was, so the least I could do was put her mind at rest.

"Good morning. I'm looking for a dog," I informed the warden of Siddingleigh Animal Home when I arrived on the Saturday.

"Then you've come to the right place! What did you have in mind? Pet? Watchdog?"

"No, no. I don't mean I'm looking for just *any* dog. I'm looking for my own dog," I explained. "It ran away last week, and I thought it might have been brought here."

The warden assumed a businesslike expression. "Oh, I see, sir. Perhaps you could give me a description of the animal?"

I racked my brains, trying to find a not-too-insulting way to describe Rover. "Well, he's sort of black and white and mangy looking, and a bit cross-eyed. Oh, and he answers to the name of Rover."

The warden raised an eyebrow. "Yes, don't they all, sir. Maybe it would be better if we just took a walk round, see if you can spot him."

I followed him out to the cages at the back of the office. There were black dogs and brown dogs, and dappled dogs; large dogs and small dogs; thoroughbreds and mongrels. About the only thing they had in common was the fact that they were all incredibly *noisy* dogs.

"No. No, he's not here," I shouted over the frantic barking, after a swift perusal had revealed no black and white dogs.

We started back towards the office, past a small row of cages separated from the rest. "That's the ones we've found homes for," the warden explained.

I gave them a cursory glance, then stopped abruptly as two luminous brown eyes almost, but not quite, met my own. There, nose against the wire netting, was a black and white and mangy-looking, mongrel.

Also very obvious was the large white label on the front of the cage. "*Sold*," it declared in bold capitals.

"Sold?" I exclaimed indignantly. "You've *sold* my dog?"

The warden began to look uncomfortable, and hastened me back into the office.

"I'm sorry, sir, but if they're not collected within seven days, we've either got to find homes for them or destroy them. Yours was bought yesterday by a — er —" he consulted a ledger on the desk in front of him "— Miss Jean Richmond. She's coming to collect him this morning. Maybe you could —"

He broke off, and peered out of the office window. "In fact, here's the young lady now, if I'm not mistaken. Perhaps I should just go and get Rover and leave the two of you to sort this out between yourselves."

Bidding a hasty "good morning" to the girl who had come in, the warden retreated to the kennels.

"Well, it's no wonder he ran away from you!" Jean Richmond exclaimed indignantly when I had politely explained the situation and offered to reimburse her for all expenses. "I saw the state that poor creature was in. It looks to me as though you've been ill-treating him!"

"*Ill-treating him!* Young lady, I'll have you know that he was in a far worse state than that when I, out of the goodness of my heart, offered him a home!"

"Then why did he run away from you?" she demanded, and shot me a triumphant look.

Fortunately, the warden's entrance with Rover saved me from thinking up a reply to that unanswerable question.

"Poor darling," the girl said, bending down to rub his ears. "Never mind, you're safe now. I'll make sure of that."

"Now just a minute!" I exclaimed. This nonsense had gone on long enough, and it was about time somebody put a stop to it. "That dog belongs to me, and he's coming back home with me right now."

"Oh no, he's not," she declared firmly. "I've paid for him, and he's coming with me. Isn't that right?"

She turned to the warden, who looked desperately from side to side, as if wondering whether or not he could escape unnoticed.

"Well?" I demanded.

He gave up thoughts of flight, and scratched his head. "Yes. Well. Difficult situation. Most difficult situation. I don't think anything like this has ever happened before."

"But now that it *has*," the girl said, "what do you intend to do about it?"

"I don't rightly know," the warden confessed. "Our policy has always been to do what's best for the dog, but in a case like this —"

He contemplated Rover, who had stretched himself out on the floor and gone to sleep, then looked up at the two of us and beamed hopefully. His next suggestion took me completely by surprise.

"Wouldn't it be a good idea if Miss Richmond took him for a week, and then returned him to you for a week, and then — and then —"

"And then what?" I inquired.

He was looking slightly less hopeful now. "Well, and then whichever of you he had got on best with could — could keep him?"

Miss Richmond and I looked uncertainly at each other for a moment.

"Well, it's not very satisfactory, but I suppose we could try it," she agreed doubtfully.

Reluctantly, I agreed and, giving Rover a quick pat, left him to the tender mercies of his new but temporary mistress.

Whatever else could be said of the formidable Miss Richmond, at least she kept her word. Promptly at eleven o'clock the following Saturday, Rover was returned to me for the second week of the trial.

"I don't know what you're making such a fuss about, Ian," my mother said when he was duly installed in his basket. "You said you only took him in because you felt sorry for him. I would have thought you'd be glad that nice young lady wanted to give him a home."

"Nice young lady, indeed!" I said. "She's a self-opinionated, pushy little madam.

"And anyway, that's not the point. It's a question of — of —"

"Pride," my mother said sharply.

I ignored that remark and got on with brushing Rover. He would certainly never make Crufts', but if my efforts had anything to do with it, then by the end of the week he would be an almost respectable representative of the canine world. And that would show Miss Know-It-All Richmond!

Malevolently, I started to look forward to my next encounter with that young lady.

Or at least I did until Wednesday.

"Where's Rover?" I asked my mother on returning from work that fateful day.

She fluttered nervously for a moment, and that gave me my first inkling of disaster.

"He — he's gone. He went out in the garden this morning, and then the next time I looked, he had just sort of — vanished."

"Vanished? But he can't have vanished. That garden is practically escape-proof!" I paused for a moment. "Unless, of course, somebody opened the gate."

"Well, don't look at me," my mother said defensively. "I certainly didn't let him out!"

"No, I know you didn't," I told her. "But there's someone else who might have. She was far too friendly when she came on Saturday. I might have known she was planning something."

"Ian, dear," my mother said patiently. "What are you talking about?"

"Kidnapping, that's what! I bet ,that devious little madam has lured him away!"

Ignoring her protests, I headed straight for the telephone.

WELL, of all the nerve!" Jean Richmond shouted into my left ear. "You drove the poor little thing away and then you've got the barefaced cheek to accuse me of abducting him!"

"If you haven't got him, then where is he?" I demanded.

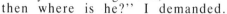

There was a pause at the other end of the line, then her voice came over, cold and condemnatory.

"That's precisely what I'd like to know," she said. "And instead of arguing like a couple of kids, we'd be better employed trying to find him. The poor mite is probably wandering about town, soaked and frozen half to death."

I glanced out of the window at the sleety rain. Why was it Rover always chose to disappear in the worst of weather?

"All right," I said reluctantly. "You take the south end, and I'll do the north. I'll meet you at the Civic Centre at nine o'clock."

Three hours, a couple of gales, and a snowstorm later, I confronted Jean Richmond at the appointed place.

"Nothing," I said, as she raised her eyebrows questioningly.

"Well, that's it, then." She shrugged. "Unless he found some shelter, he's had it. He couldn't possibly survive this."

Judging from Jean's appearance, neither could she, and I put aside ill-feeling and offered her a lift home.

"I don't suppose he could have been picked up by the dog-catcher again, could he?" she said as we got into the car.

I glanced at my watch. It was well after closing time, but the warden lived on the premises and might just be available.

Jean looked hopefully at me, and I nodded. After all, the home was only five minutes' drive away.

"I was wondering when you two would appear." The warden greeted us with a smile as he opened the front door. "He came in on the four o'clock van. Hang on a minute and I'll get him."

"So much for him being frozen half to death," I said sourly, when he returned with the happy wanderer. "He's sitting here, warm as toast, while we've practically got pneumonia!"

Jean shot me a cold look, our earlier truce now forgotten.

"That's just what I would have expected of you. Don't you ever think about anyone but yourself?" Her look was icy.

She turned to the warden and smiled. "Well, I think that settles once and for all the question of Rover's permanent home. He was obviously trying to find his way back to me when he ran off."

"Certainly looks like it," the warden agreed. "What do you say, Mr Craig?"

As the only thing I felt like saying would not have been fit for a lady's ears. I refrained from saying anything at all. Perhaps Rover and Jean Richmond deserved each other, I decided. They were both ill-mannered, ungrateful wretches, and I wished them joy together.

"I wonder how they're getting on?" my mother said suddenly the following week.

"Who?" I asked.

She tutted. "You know perfectly well who I mean, Ian. You've been brooding about it all week.

"In fact," she went on, eyeing me in that way mothers have, "I'm beginning to wonder just which of them it is you're missing."

"What's that supposed to mean?" I demanded, but she was saved the trouble of replying when the doorbell rang.

I went to answer it, and found Jean Richmond poised awkwardly on the doorstep.

"Er, sorry to bother you, Mr Craig," she began falteringly, "but I was wondering if Rover was here?"

I surveyed for a moment, swallowing the ungentlemanly cackle of triumph that threatened to burst from my lips.

Instead, I managed a small, restrained smile. "How long's he been missing this time?"

"Since yesterday morning." She had the grace to blush. "He took off. I thought maybe he'd come back here."

"Well, he hasn't," I retorted. "But I've a pretty good idea where he will be!"

W E drove the three miles in a silence that was only broken when we reached Siddingleigh Dog's Home.
"Well?" I demanded of the warden.
He nodded. "He came in last night."

"Well, at least he's safe," Jean said thankfully. "I suppose that's something. But if he runs away from both of us, what are we going to do about it? We still don't know who he prefers to live with."

"Of course we do," the warden announced, and I stared up at him.

"Who?" Jean demanded.

"Me," he said smugly. "Looks like your wild Rover was running with a pack while he was a stray. He misses the company of other dogs, so he chases after the dog-catcher's van so's he'll get brought back here.

"Quite smart of him, really," he went on admiringly. "I've been thinking I'll keep him myself. Always did have a soft spot for intelligent animals."

I turned to Jean, but found that she was no more capable of speech than I was myself. For once we were on an equal footing!

"Well, of all the —" I tried eventually, but spluttered to a stop.

"Quite," she said succinctly. "I think we've both had a lucky escape, Ian. There's obviously a nasty, twisted, perverse streak in that dog."

"Definitely," I agreed. "It should have been obvious right away. One of nature's misfits if ever I saw one."

The warden frowned indignantly. "Perverse, my foot! If anyone's perverse, it's you pair. Practically at each other's throat over a poor little dog.

"Now, if you don't mind —" he got to his feet —– "I've got work to be getting on with."

I held the door for Jean, and together we walked over towards the side gate where I had left my car.

"At each other's throats, indeed!" I said. "We weren't, were we?"

"Of course not, Ian," she assured me. "That man is just trying to stir up trouble. And I didn't think for a moment that you had really ill-treated Rover. You're obviously much too nice."

I beamed at her. "And I was only joking when I accused you of kidnapping him. The very idea is ludicrous."

We stopped in front of the last cage, and I put a hand on her shoulder. "But just to show there's no hard feelings, what about having dinner with me tonight?"

"That would be lovely. Maybe we could go —"

She broke off as a whine came from the occupant of the cage.

"Oh, Ian, look! Isn't he adorable!"

I poked a finger through the wire and let the tiny, sandy-coloured pup lick it gently.

"Looks as if he's part Labrador," I said, kneeling down to get a closer look. "I've always had a thing about Labradors. And really, when you come to think of it, it's much more sensible to get a puppy instead of a full-grown dog like Rover, who's already set in his ways. This little fellow would be perfect."

Jean glared at me. "Now just a minute. I saw him first. If that puppy isn't claimed, then I'm having him!"

I glared back. "Who says? Anyway, you didn't see him first. We both saw him at the same time, so if he's not claimed we'll have to toss for it. Right?"

Eventually, that's just what we did.

Honey is almost two now, one of the healthiest, most alert and energetic young dogs I have ever seen.

But there are times when I wish that coin hadn't landed on "heads."

Like tonight for instance, when it's wet and cold and miserable, and Honey is demanding his two-mile walk.

"I don't suppose you'd like to take him?" I ask my wife.

"Certainly not!" Jean, curled up in front of the fire, smiles superciliously at me.

"After all, he's your dog. You won the toss!" □

For the first time ever, she hadn't bought her husband a birthday present. Her excuse? She'd been . . .

Otherwise Engaged

HOW noisy my surroundings are — but pleasantly noisy. Comforting, like a thick, fleecy blanket on a cold night. I can hear the happy sound of people talking, the low humming of the busy traffic, filtering through.

Comfortable, I'll let my thoughts float me along, till you arrive, Gary . . .

Today is a special day. The calendar hanging up in the kitchen has a large red cross on it, made with a felt-tipped pen. I always mark important occasions like that, with red ink, in case I forget something.

But today isn't likely to slip my mind. Gary, you're thirty-three today.

You don't look your age. I've got a picture of you which I carry around with me. It's in my head. A face that isn't good looking in the conventional way, but strong featured.

The French have a word for it. *Joli-laid* — ugly-attractive.

Dear Gary, if only you knew how much I care, deep down inside. The years haven't diminished my love for you, only added to it.

You grow more precious to me as each year goes by, and even now I marvel at the idea that someone as wonderful as you could want anyone as ordinary as me.

Another birthday, Gary. Many happy returns.

I've bought you loads of presents since we've been together, haven't I? Expensive gifts, when we were feeling well off, which wasn't very often! And the little tiny nonsenses when we were broke.

They gave me so much pleasure, all of them, the choosing, the buying and the wrapping up.

I can almost read the story of our marriage in those parcels. We've had ten years together, ten years of changes, big and small, but I haven't changed at all.

You see, I've always been awkward, timid, always afraid of saying the wrong thing. And I've always taken a child-like delight in the silly little pleasures of life, that others would brush scornfully aside.

Like your birthday presents.

I wonder which one gave *you* the most pleasure? I hope you enjoyed them all, because, you see, I haven't bought you one this year.

I feel really bad about it, but I haven't had the chance to go shopping — everything has happened unexpectedly, and my plans have all flown out of the window.

I did manage to get you a card, but I'm afraid it's only one of those insulting ones in a long, thin envelope.

D

OTHERWISE ENGAGED

Cards are a symbol to me. Like the silly little presents I gave you when the piggy bank was empty.

Only one thing has ever been missing from our lives — the baby we've longed for so much, and nothing else could take the place of that.

THE years are blurring, Gary, and suddenly I'm twelve years younger.

Remember your twenty-first birthday? It was our engagement party as well.

You've still got that battered briefcase in the loft, the one you file old bills in.

It was new and shiny when I bought it for you, ready for your new shiny job. You had a tiny pay packet, and mounds of studying.

Three years later, we were just-marrieds, the extravagant honeymoon in Paris over — living in a rented flat in the not-so-smart end of town.

I get a little wistful when I think of those pinch-penny days. The fun, the laughter, the looking forward, the never-ending cauliflower cheeses for supper, and the home-made wine that didn't always turn out quite right.

And our smiles of congratulation, when friends acquired washing machines and colour televisions, while we were still painfully trying to save a house deposit.

That first lean year, there hadn't been really anything to spare for a birthday present. But for a joke I got you a little teddy bear, only three inches high.

Do you remember your mascot, sitting on your desk, and passing all your exams for you?

Then — somehow we'd managed to scrape together enough money for a deposit on that tiny terraced cottage.

It was fearfully old, but it was home. A love nest we didn't have to share with a nagging landlady.

Only the huge mortgage repayments. But at least we could shut our very own front door and laugh at the bills.

You were so very practical that year. You insisted on a new pair of jeans. Your existing pair were almost transparent with wear, but you wore them when building, banging in nails, painting anything that would stand still for five minutes.

And remember when you got bitten by the camera bug? Our poor little spare room was filled from floor to ceiling with your bits of junk, with lines of drying prints draped everywhere like wet washing.

I bought you all the gear while we could afford it, because we'd decided to start a family.

But the house was so small, and wasn't really in the sort of area where we wanted to bring up a child. I was spending all my time, very broodily, looking in the estate agents' windows.

Back to saving hard again, then all that dreadful upheaval of moving.

Another birthday, and a beautiful new house the very same day. And several tins of lemon-coloured paint to decorate the nursery.

You were doing so well at the office. We had a lovely home. The stage was set, but one of the actors didn't know her part and the nursery stayed empty.

I told myself not to worry about her absence — I'd set my heart upon a little girl. Babies didn't come to order out of one of those glossy mail-order catalogues.

But the missing piece of the jigsaw upset you far more, Gary.

We'd been together for five years then, a long time to stay in love by modern standards.

The doctor didn't seem to think it was a long time, though. There was nothing wrong with either of us — just relax and stop trying so hard. The words came easily to him, he said them every day, but he didn't have to *live* with them.

So I treated you to a late — very late! — birthday present, skiing in the Italian Alps. I half hoped the holiday would have to be cancelled because I was pregnant.

Jeff and Brenda had to drop their plans to go to Greece a few months earlier for that reason and I had hoped it was catching.

But eventually, weary of living in hope, we put the family idea right out of our heads.

Lots of people didn't bother nowadays, I convinced you, with a brightness I didn't feel inside.

YOU got your big chance just after all that, didn't you? Promotion, and the pay that went with it, and moving house again.

This time the house was detached, with a huge garden, and very glossy neighbours. I was grateful for my senior secretary's job, just so that we could keep up with their standard of living.

Every single family on that estate had hundreds of pounds worth of hi-fi, so that's what I bought for you that year.

And I carefully cultivated an air of superiority about my job, as I was the only working wife in the neighbourhood. I managed to fool our friends and acquaintances, but I couldn't kid myself.

I wasn't the original Career Girl. I would have given anything to have been tied to the sink and a pile of nappies by my apron strings.

Sadly, I watched all my friends buying cuddly toys for their babies, and all I could do was buy things for you instead.

The next few years ran away, like the crystal water of a swift-flowing stream. Our love was still there, but where, oh where, had the time gone?

The nursery stayed empty, because I hadn't the heart to strip off the wallpaper with its pattern of tiny kittens. Every now and then, I would go in there, and feel their big round eyes watching me.

You felt left out at the office when your staff laughed and talked about their kids' progress. I knew you felt it even more than I did.

Continued on page 55.

A Cosy

Cover

Materials Required — Of Patons Bee-hive Tumble Dry Double Knit, 2 x 50 gram balls in each of main and contrast colours; one pair each of 3¼ mm and 4 mm (Nos. 10 and 8) knitting needles.

Quantities of yarn stated are based on average requirements and are therefore approximate.

For best results it is essential to use the recommended yarn. If you have difficulty in obtaining the yarn, write direct, enclosing a stamped addressed envelope, to the following address for stockists: Consumer Services Department, Coats Patons Crafts, McMullen Road, Darlington, Co. Durham DL1 1YQ. Tel: 0325 381010.

Measurement — To fit large-size teapot.

Tension — 11 stitches and 15 rows to 5 centimetres, *2 inches*, measured over stocking-stitch using 4 mm needles.

If your tension is too tight, try a size larger needles. If it is too loose, try a size smaller.

Abbreviations — K — knit; st.(s) — stitch(es); tog. — together; M — main; C — contrast.

N.B. Pleats are formed by each colour being drawn across back of colour just used and keeping all strands to wrong side throughout.

With 3¼ mm needles and M, cast on 98 sts. and knit 5 rows.

Change to 4 mm needles, join in C and work in pattern as follows:

1st row — K1M, 6C, *7M, 7C; repeat from * to last 7 sts., 6M, 1C.

2nd row — K1C, 6M, *7C, 7M; repeat from * to last 7 sts., 6C, 1M.

3rd to 6th rows — As 1st and 2nd rows twice more.

7th row — K1C, 6M, *7C, 7M; repeat from * to last 7 sts., 6C, 1M.

8th row — K1M, 6C, *7M, 7C; repeat from * to last 7 sts., 6M, 1C.

9th to 12th rows — As 7th and 8th rows twice more.

These 12 rows form pattern.

Repeat them 4 times more.

Shape Top

Next row — K2 tog.M, K3C, K2 tog.C, *K2 tog.M, K3M, K2 tog.M, K2 tog.C, K3C, K2 tog.C; repeat from * to last 7 sts., K2 tog.M, K3M, K2 tog.C.

Next row — K1C, 4M, *5C, 5M; repeat from * to last 5 sts., 4C, 1M.

Next row — K2 tog.M, K1C, K2 tog.C, *K2 tog.M, K1M, K2 tog.M, K2 tog.C, K1C, K2 tog. C; repeat from * to last 5 sts., K2 tog.M, K1M, K2 tog. C.

Next row — K1C, 2M, *3C, 3M; repeat from * to last 3 sts., 2C, 1M.

Next row — K2 tog.M, K1C, *K2 tog.M, K1M, K2 tog.C., K1C; repeat from * to last 3 sts., K2 tog.M, K1C.

Next row — K1C, 1M, *2C, 2M; repeat from * to last 2 sts., 1C, 1M.

Next row — [K2 tog.M] twice, *K2 tog.C., K2 tog.M; repeat from * to last 4 sts., [K2 tog.C] twice.

Break off yarns, thread end of C through remaining sts., draw up and fasten off.

Make 2nd half the same.

TO MAKE UP

Stitch side and top seams leaving openings for handle and spout.

With C, make 3 pom-poms and sew to top of cosy.

With 2 strands M, crochet a chain and tie in loops on top. □

Continued from page 51.

Why did I ever mention adoption? That sparked off the one and only row we ever had. I never thought you were capable of such a frightening temper. Soft, kind-hearted Gary, who wouldn't hurt a fly.

But afterwards, I knew the reason why, even though you never told me.

You felt a failure, didn't you?

And someone else's child wouldn't have eased that pain.

That killed my last, lingering hopes stone dead.

Besides, weren't we too set in our ways by then? A baby would only have caused upheaval. We used any excuse to hide the pain.

Last year, you got a bee in your bonnet about sailing. Just because you'd read about people going round the world single handed.

I wasn't enthusiastic about boats. I could swim — if I had to. But the only water I liked messing about in was warm and scented, with the promise of a fluffy bath-towel afterwards.

So instead of a baby we had a boat.

But why did you have to call her Marianne? That was what we'd happily chosen from the book of babies' names, so long ago. If we'd had a girl.

Dreams, dreams, and you still carried them with you, in white letters on the blue fibreglass hull.

★   ★   ★   . ★

I could carry on day-dreaming for the rest of today — but a car has suddenly backfired outside the window and startles me out of my reverie.

Where have the years gone? Where have the hours gone? I look at the clock. Almost time. Just a few minutes and you'll be here.

A little sigh escapes my lips. Almost as if in gratitude for the happiness we've shared, in spite of the dull ache of childlessness nagging away at us.

Lots of our friends have managed to get everything they've ever wanted — families, nice houses, money, yet they've ended up bitterly wrangling in the divorce courts.

At least you and I have something precious, something that all the troubles in the world can't destroy. We've stuck together for better, for worse . . .

"Mrs Watkins, here's your husband now," the nurse says.

I'm smiling at you through a mist of happy tears.

"Here's your present, darling. Happy birthday . . ."

I'm the happiest woman in the ward, as I hold our brand new baby daughter, Marianne. □

Up, Up And

Ever wished you could fly away from it all? Then take a trip with Caroline who really did. (Honest!)

By JANE O'HARE

WASHDAY was always like this. A muddle. Toast crumbs and spilled sugar on the kitchen table, the water in the washing machine bubbling and steaming, misting the windows and dimming her view of the garden.

Today the wind was high, bending the rose bushes towards the East, blustering a mass of gold-tinged clouds across the sky like a herd of sheep. A west wind; damp, so that it wouldn't dry the clothes quickly and rough enough to wrap the sheets infuriatingly around the line.

Caroline sighed as she cleared the dishes from the table into the sink, and squirted washing-up liquid into the bowl. Oh, not to have to wash again, ever! Oh, not to have to rinse, and shake, and peg out!

Then she pursed her lips ruefully, because it was ungrateful to feel that way. When the children had been babies they hadn't been able to afford a washing machine. She hadn't even had a garden to peg out in, either. Then, it had been soak, boil, rinse, and hand-wring.

It was much easier now. Just load, unload, spin, rinse, and peg

Away

out. But it was still washing, and she hated it.

She peered up at the window. The top panes were only misted in the centre, and she could watch the scudding cloud parade, and see red-tiled rooftops.

Chimneys, and TV aerials, and birds sailing like leaves on that buffeting wind. Sailing free!

She leaned against the sink, dish mop dripping into the bowl, and sighed again, wistfully. There was something about far-off rooftops, chimney pots, and high torn clouds that excited her. Exhilarated her. She used to yearn, when she was a child, to plane on the wind like a bird, or to dance on the rooftops.

A child's silly fancy. She returned to the washing-up.

The washer took two cotton sheets at a time, but Granny's sheet had to go in by itself, because it was good old-fashioned twill.

A double sheet it was, almost. Home made, hand stitched and

nearly indestructible.

It was at least fifty years old, and must have been a horror to struggle through a mangle. Even the spin-drier groaned and whistled at it.

The sheet had belonged to Granny Davis, then to Caroline's mother, and now it was hers. It might even survive to pass on to eight-year-old Diana, when or if she married.

It was a blessing in winter, for it tucked far beneath the mattress, never budging, not letting a whisper of draught enter to chill the bed.

Granny Davis used to thumb it clean with her washing-dolly, and Mother used to stab it down hard into her wash boiler. Nowadays, Caroline simply grabbed it with the tongs, and eased it from tub to spin-drier.

Two good rinses, and pump the water away. Then the sheet came spilling out into the waiting basket, still full of wear, still white as snow.

She put more washing into the machine, then carried the sheet outside by itself. It needed eight pegs to secure it to the clothes line. The first time she'd washed it she'd only used three, and it had flapped itself free, to whirl across the garden and land slap in the mud of the children's digging hole.

Now she caught up the four corners in a bunch in her left hand, some pegs ready in her right. The wind came swooping down around her, pressing her clothes against her body, and, finding the sheet, forced its way inside, quested around, and formed a balloon.

The balloon grew larger as the wind found it was trapped, and she dropped the pegs, to cling on with both hands.

The wind was as strong as a herd of horses, pouring into the sheet balloon. It strained wildly to go on its way, but she wouldn't let go. Like a primitive, captured beast, it fought to get out, and it fought to go upwards.

Slowly the sheet balloon began to rise, and because Caroline wouldn't let go, she began to rise, too.

She rose first to her toe-tips, her arms drawn up to their limit, and for a long, battling moment her body was a link between earth and sky.

Then the wind triumphed, and her toes left the ground. She was dangling in space, one inch above the grass, then five, a foot! It was delightful!

But she had to let go — now, or now, or now!

She didn't let go. And then, suddenly, it was too late, because she was a good five feet up, and rising fast.

HAVING won the battle, the wind was her master. Now it could take her higher and higher; it could whirl her wherever it would.

After the first gasping moments of unbelief and resistance, Caroline loved it. The sun glinted and twinkled on the window panes of her home, and she noted, as she floated past, that her net curtains needed washing again. Also, in the gutter near Tony's bedroom, she saw that blue plastic ball he'd lost last year.

Those gutters needed scraping, she decided, and some of the tiles were loose.

She peered downwards as she passed high over the fence, and was floated across her neighbour's garden. Val Tovey was pegging out, and didn't glance up. She *was* dyeing her hair! As the wind tossed her blonde curls about, the black roots were quite plain.

Why did Val fib about it? Caroline wondered, as she drifted onwards. Blonde hair suited Val anyway, she had a fair skin.

Ah! John Tovey *had* broken Richard's garden roller when he'd borrowed it last autumn. She could see it in their greenhouse, and the handle was off.

Yet John kept saying to Richard, "I'll bring it round, sorry I keep forgetting. But it's OK in our greenhouse, isn't it? You won't need it yet, will you?"

The wind tugged her away from the Toveys', and she had to raise her feet slightly or her toes would have tapped on their tiles. Next door's tiles, she appraised, were in a worse state than her own. Perhaps it would be a good idea to suggest going halves on having them seen to?

Those red rooftops were getting closer, and she smiled with pleased anticipation. Two birds, fluttering past, dropped like stones when they saw her; quite shocked.

Below, the streets were blue-grey ribbons, the Monday traffic mainly heavy goods vehicles, hindered in some places by milk floats and a very few cars. Housewives in Minis, dodging the Monday wash for a spot of window shopping, perhaps?

No-one looked upwards. Odd, but people rarely did look up these days. They were all so tensely engrossed with daily life.

Gardens were far nicer from above, she thought, as she travelled away from the town. It was lovely, picking out the patterns they made from her present viewpoint. Square lawns, diamonds, oblongs, crazy paving; what splendid imagination it showed.

If only their owners and tenders could see them from here, how thrilled they'd be! How delighted that their own small patch of land, added to all the others, made a wide and beautiful carpet under the heavens.

Now here were rooftops again, where she ought to raise her feet, but still — just one or two taps!

The wind wove the sheet balloon in and out amongst the chimney pots, and her toes danced and danced, and her heart, which had yearned for this years ago, danced too. Free, free as a bird planing on the wind, free as air . . .

The wind was beginning to lose strength now, and little spots of rain flecked the tiles, yet Granny's sheet knew its way home. Probably because it had served the family too long not to? The wind had just enough energy left to lower her down on to the lawn, and then, with a sigh, subside out of the balloon, and whisper away across the grass.

"I shouldn't bother to peg that out, if I were you," Val called from a bedroom window. "The wind's dropped. It's spitting with rain, too. I've fetched my washing in."

Caroline stood with the sheet limp in her hands, as Val added. "Too strong to last, that wind. Blew itself out."

"Yes," Caroline replied regretfully. "It was too good to last."

As she lifted the basket she called to Val, "Come round for a coffee, if you've time. I want to have a word with you about something."

"Anything special?" Val asked.

"The roof tiles, for one thing —" Caroline said. And the garden roller for another, she thought.

As she walked back to the house and the washing, she reflected that it was indeed an ill wind that blew nobody any good at all . . . □

Complete Story By
BETTY HAWORTH

**Simple, wasn't it?
All she had to do
was tell her
daughters she'd
fallen in love . . .**

the
trouble with
LOVE

61

THE TROUBLE WITH LOVE

A S soon as she came into the kitchen, Fran knew the girls had been arguing again. Barbara's face was flushed and Chris wore the stubborn look that seemed to be her permanent expression these days.

Fran sat down with the morning paper and poured herself a cup of coffee, while the silence between her daughters grew more and more uncomfortable. She knew if she went out the argument would begin again.

"Come along now, girls!" she said quietly. "It's rather early in the day to be falling out, don't you think?"

Barbara rose to her feet, trim and smart in her nurse's uniform. She looked a little shamefaced, but Chris continued to stare down at her plate, her face defiant.

"Sorry, Mum!" Barbara said, bending to kiss her mother quickly. "I must go. See you tonight."

"Yes," Fran said, smiling at her.

Barbara picked up her mac and her navy shoulder-bag, and a moment later they heard the front door close behind her.

Fran looked despairingly across the table at her younger daughter. Chris was sitting with her elbows on the cloth staring into her cup of cold coffee. Her hair was a mess, and Fran could see the heavy eye make-up she wore these days had not been washed off before she went to bed. Not surprising, considering the time she had come in the previous night.

"Chris? I do wish you'd tell me what's wrong! You know I — "

But Chris got up from the table abruptly, her breakfast untouched. Fran listened to her getting ready for school, the banging of drawers, feet coming angrily downstairs. Then the front door slammed, and she was gone, without even calling goodbye.

Fran sat and looked out of the kitchen window. Life had become so different and so complicated ever since she had fallen in love.

That was the trouble with love, she thought sadly. Love might be the sweetest thing, and make the world go round, but it was also worrying and exasperating and fraught with difficulties — especially when you were a widow of forty-six with two teenage daughters.

Paul had come into her life so quietly, so unexpectedly, and every single day that passed made her marvel at her good fortune. She had been alone for so long that she had honestly believed herself to be used to loneliness, contented in a way and self-sufficient.

How foolish she had been! Paul had walked into her life and turned it upside down. She had discovered that she was lonely, and that she was capable of falling in love again after all these years with all the agony and ecstasy of a girl.

Fran sighed. Paul had asked her to marry him more than a month ago, and she had longed to say yes at once. But she had hesitated, thinking of what it would mean — thinking especially about the girls.

She had told Paul about her fears.

"They're still so young, Paul, especially Chris. I know Barbara has a responsible job at the hospital, but that's the very reason why she needs me. She takes things to heart, and there are exams coming up soon.

"She wants so much to make a success of her career, and she cares so much about the future. She must feel that I'm there when she needs me."

"But you will be there!" Paul had protested. "We both will! I don't want to take you away from the girls, you mustn't think that."

"And Chris," Fran said. "She's still a child in so many ways, in spite of the make-up and the boys. Seventeen is such a vulnerable age, and she's going through a difficult patch just now.

"There's something troubling her and I can't find out what it is. She hardly speaks these days, and I honestly don't know what she would say about us getting married."

"Ask her then," Paul had suggested reasonably. "We get on all right — I mean, as well as anyone gets on with Chris at the moment!"

"I mustn't do anything to upset her."

"She's upsetting you," Paul said. "It might do her good to see that you have some feelings too, and a right to a life of your own. Put yourself first for a change, Fran! You're not afraid to tell her, are you?"

Fran had laughed, a little shamefacedly. "Barbara will give me moral support! I would have told Barbara about us weeks ago, but I didn't feel it was fair to tell one and not the other."

"No, you must tell them together," Paul had agreed. "And Barbara will give you a pat and say: Well done, Mother! Just what the doctor ordered! and we'll have to arrange the wedding to coincide with her weekend off."

Fran gazed absently out at the garden. Dear Paul! If only she could tell him she would marry him right away, and be sure that everything would work out.

But there was this niggling uncertainty about Chris, the fear that she would do something silly and impulsive — like leaving school this summer and going into some dead-end job. She had talked about that recently, and about leaving home and going to live in a flat. Perhaps her mother's remarriage would provide the excuse she wanted?

And yet Fran knew her daughter so well. Chris was deeply unhappy about something. The hurtful things she said and did were only the outwards signs of an inward discontent.

Barbara had seemed to get through her adolescent years with little trouble, but poor Chris was learning the hard way how incredibly painful the transition from child to woman could be.

A tap on the kitchen door startled her.

"Good morning, Mrs Mitchell! I hope you're daydreaming about me?"

"Oh, Paul!" Fran said, her eyes filling with tears.

"What's wrong?"

THE TROUBLE WITH LOVE

"Nothing. No, it's nothing really . . ."

"You mean just the usual things?"

She nodded, and he held her hands very tightly. "Marry me, Fran," he said softly. "And then I can worry for both of us."

"This is something I have to work out for myself. But I can't see any way round it at the moment."

"Look," he said, "there is a way round. You're going to tell those girls of yours that you've fallen in love, and

we're going to get married. It's quite simple really. And then we're going to live happily ever after!"

Fran smiled in spite of herself. "You make it sound so easy," she said. "But for me it's not."

He leaned across the table and kissed her gently. "Stop worrying," he told her. "Next weekend I'm going to take you over to Millford to look at those new houses, and when you've found one you like we'll tell the girls they're going to live in the country."

"Millford!" Fran exclaimed. "You mean those lovely detached houses near the golf course? But, Paul — "

"No buts," he said.

"Darling," Fran said, joy and excitement flooding through her. "You're wonderful."

"I'm determined too," he warned her. "As Miss Christine Mitchell is going to find out very soon. There'll be no more talking about leaving school when she's my daughter, and she'll start eating proper meals and combing her hair."

"You're going to have an awful struggle!" Fran smiled at him.

"Never mind about that," he said firmly. "She'll be outnumbered and in time you and I and Barbara will turn her into a reasonable human being, won't we?"

"Yes, Paul," Fran said meekly. "Whatever you say!"

FRAN went shopping and had her hair done. In the evening, she started the meal early, set the table with her best china and cutlery and put a little posy of flowers in the centre. Then she changed into a pretty skirt and top and took a last, satisfied look at the table.

Everything would be all right, she told herself. She had been worrying too much about Chris, and about a lot of other things too, but now she was going to be sensible. All that really mattered was that Paul loved her.

Fran looked at the clock anxiously at half-past five. Chris was usually home long before now, and she hadn't said anything about staying late at school. Then she remembered how Chris had slammed out of the house that morning without a word, and a little chill stole over her.

At six o'clock Barbara's voice called cheerfully from the hall.

"I'm home, Mum! What a gorgeous smell. Is it something special?" She came into the kitchen.

"Hello, dear!" Fran said cheerfully. "It's only chicken but I've made a special stuffing and some sauce with cream."

"Clever girl!" Barbara kissed her. "What are we celebrating?"

Fran, ridiculously, felt nervous, and even a little shy.

"I'll tell you when Chris arrives."

"Where is she? It's gone six."

"Probably staying late at school," Fran said lightly. "Music Club or something."

"Didn't she tell you?"

"Well, no. But — "

"No, she wouldn't!" Barbara said grimly. "She treats her home as if it were a hotel these days! If Chris can't have the manners to tell you when she's coming in for meals then she'll have to do without!"

She went to wash, and Fran stood in the kitchen alone. She felt her happy excitement ebbing away, with the fading light outside. She had been too optimistic. Whether she married Paul or not, whether they moved to a lovely new home or not, would make no difference. Chris didn't care. As soon as she was old enough she would go away and make her own life somewhere else.

SHAKING herself, Fran turned to serve the meal, and carried the dishes through to the dining-room.

"We'll have ours," she told Barbara, trying to sound cheerful. "There's something important I want to tell you and I can't wait any longer. Paul said I should tell you together, but if Chris — "

"Paul?" Barbara said, looking up quickly.

Fran put down the dishes and sat down calmly, enjoying Barbara's complete attention. "Help yourself to vegetables, dear."

Barbara sat still. "What about Paul?"

"Oh, he's asked me to marry him and I've said yes," Fran said lightly.

There was a long silence. She looked up, and laughed at Barbara's stunned expression.

"Well, don't look like that!"

"You hardly know him, Mother!"

Fran's smile faded slowly as she recognised the shock in her daughter's face.

"What do you mean? We've known one another for months!"

Barbara looked away quickly. "Yes, I know, but I never thought . . ."

Fran went on staring at her daughter. Everything seemed suddenly to have become unreal. Her hands were cold, and when she spoke her own voice sounded distant and odd.

THE TROUBLE WITH LOVE

"What's so surprising about me wanting to get married again?" she asked. "I thought you liked Paul?"

"Well, yes — but that's not the point," Barbara began.

"That's exactly the point, I should have thought." Fran got up from the table and moved away, until the silence between them grew unbearable.

"I never thought you'd take it like this, Barbara. I never dreamed that you . . ."

"Take it like what?" Barbara broke in, her voice trembling.

"I thought you'd be glad — happy for me. I was relying on that."

"I'm only thinking about you, Mother," Barbara said shakily.

Fran turned and stared at her.

"No," she said. "You're thinking about yourself. You want things to go on in the way they always have, don't you? You're just thinking about the effect this will have on your well-organised life!"

"Don't get upset, Mother," Barbara whispered.

"And when I tell Chris I expect her reaction will be the same! I seem to have brought up two rather selfish people."

"You're getting things out of proportion."

"Am I?" Fran asked. "That's the trouble with love, Barbara. It seems so simple, and then you find it's not."

"Let's leave it for now," Barbara said. "You're getting upset and it won't do any good arguing."

"This is unbelievable!" Fran's eyes filled with tears. "My own daughter, and you're talking to me as though we were strangers!"

Barbara's young face was set and she avoided her mother's eyes.

"What will Chris say?" she asked stiffly.

"I don't care what Chris says!" Fran cried. "She doesn't seem to care about anyone else any more.

"I'm thinking about myself now, Barbara, for the first time in years. Paul wants to buy one of those beautiful houses at Millford, and I want to marry him and start a new life.

"I'm tired of being lonely and worried. I want to have someone to depend on, someone to lean on for a change!"

"You should have said this before." Barbara's voice was barely above a whisper. "This concerns me as well, you know. I don't want to go and live at Millford, Mother. This is my home!"

Fran looked through the tears at the trim figure in her blue uniform, proud when she remembered how caring and compassionate Barbara was in her job.

But the air of brisk efficiency with which, professionally, she covered her feelings, was gone now. Suddenly Fran saw not the dedicated nurse, but a vulnerable eighteen-year-old.

Barbara was not just surprised at her mother's news, but hurt — and could it possibly be . . . afraid?

"Barbara? What is it? What's the matter, darling?"

Her daughter flinched away, and went to stand by the window, looking out at the dark garden and the lighted windows in the road.

"Please, Barbara, please tell me what's wrong!"

There was a long silence, and then Barbara turned and looked at her mother steadily. Her voice was quiet and controlled, but there were tears on her face.

"How could you, Mummy? How could you think of getting married again after being so happy with Daddy?"

The words struck Fran like a physical blow. Barbara had not called her Mummy for years, not since she was a tiny girl, and they had all been so happy together.

Here, in this house, where even then Barbara had played hospitals with her dolls, and Chris had been a round, rosy baby who seemed to laugh all the day long! Wonderful, happy days that Fran had thought would last for ever: days that she had shut out of her mind deliberately because of the pain their memories brought her.

"Barbara," she said softly. "You mustn't be upset. I couldn't bear that! I think I can guess how you feel, but I also think you're old enough to understand.

"I loved your father deeply, darling, and that love is something I shall always have and remember — a love that belongs to me alone, that no-one can take away from me.

"I've been lonely, love, but I've had you and Chris and I've done the best I could for you. Now I have Paul. Because I want to marry him and try to make him happy, it doesn't mean that I've forgotten that other love. Please try to understand."

But Barbara turned away.

"I can't!" she said. "I can't understand!"

Fran waited a moment, and then quietly left the room. She tried to calm herself. Upstairs, she had a shower, dried her hair half-heartedly and went to bed.

She was utterly tired. Tired of worrying about other people, tired of trying to do the right thing. In bed she cried, even though she knew it would do no good, and then fell into a restless doze, waking suddenly to find that it was nearly eleven o'clock.

SHE could hear someone moving about in the hall. She slipped out of bed and went out on to the landing. Chris was coming softly upstairs still wearing her outdoor things. She stopped when she saw her mother waiting.

They looked at each other without speaking. Fran could read nothing in her face: neither defiance nor apology. In silence, she went back into her room and closed the door.

She lay and stared into the darkness; eleven o'clock and Chris had only just come in! Where had she been, who had she been with?

She tried to go back to sleep, but her mind churned this way and that in an endless repetition of worry and heart-searching. She felt confused, bitterly lonely and worst of all almost trapped.

Then she heard the bedroom door open cautiously, and turned to see Chris silhouetted against the light from the landing.

She knew at once there was something wrong: Chris hadn't been into her room for weeks. She put out her hand to switch on the

THE TROUBLE WITH LOVE

bedside light, but Chris said:

"No — don't put the lamp on!" She stood near the bed.

"Are you all right, Mother?"

"Yes — yes, of course!" Fran said quickly. "It's awfully late, Chris, where . . ."

"You've been crying, haven't you?"

The question coming from Chris was so unexpected that it took Fran's breath away.

Chris sat down on the bed, and Fran leaned over and put on the light. She was pale, and had an air of untidy dejection that tugged at Fran's heart.

Scarcely daring to hope what would come of this, Fran looked straight into her daughter's eyes.

"Yes," she said. "Yes, I've been crying."

"What about?"

"All kinds of things, but mostly because Paul's asked me to marry him and I don't know if I should."

"Why not?"

"Because of you and Barbara."

Chris's steady gaze didn't falter. In that moment Fran saw just how much her younger daughter had changed — how sad she looked, and yet how grown up! She felt a moment's grief for the little girl who had once been hers, and who would never really be hers again.

"What's that got to do with us?" Chris asked. "It's your life. People should do what they want with their own lives."

"Sometimes they can't." Fran felt the tears rushing back. "Sometimes it isn't as simple as that."

"We're grown up now, Mother," Chris said gently. "Go and be happy with Paul. You deserve it."

Fran leaned forward and looked searchingly into her daughter's tired face.

"What is it, love? What's making you unhappy?"

"Nothing." Chris shrugged. "Not now. It's all over — finished."

"Please tell me," Fran said. "You must always tell me when you're unhappy. That's what I'm here for."

"You don't want to hear about my silly mistakes." Chris smiled wryly. "I expect I'll fall in and out of love a dozen times before I'm through!"

She turned her head away, her chin raised defiantly. How easy it would be, Fran thought, for me to laugh and say that it doesn't matter — that she's too young to really be in love and that she'll find someone else when she's older, when she knows what love is really all about. And how cruel and heartless that would be, too.

It was just as possible to fall in love at seventeen as it was at forty-six, just as bewildering and painful, just as real . . .

"Life's terribly complicated, isn't it?" Chris sighed.

"Terribly," Fran agreed. "But you'll survive. You've been hurt this time, but one day you'll find someone who's right for you."

"Like Paul," Chris said shyly. "He's right for you, Mother. Kind, patient, funny . . . the sort of person who makes life seem brighter just by being there."

Fran nodded in silence, and suddenly they were smiling at each other. How wise you are, young Chris, Fran thought. And how quickly you're learning!

She looked down at her hands for a moment.

"Barbara doesn't seem very happy about me getting married," she said cheerfully. "She can't understand how I can be in love . . . with someone else . . . after Daddy."

"Barbara is impertinent," Chris said calmly, and Fran glanced up at her in surprise.

"It has nothing at all to do with Barbara. Or with me either. Love isn't something you measure out, so much and no more, is it?"

Chris smiled suddenly. "What does Barbara know about falling in love anyway? Barbara's in love with her job! When she dies — having first donated her body to medical science, of course — I bet they'll find 'Sterile Container' written on her heart."

They both began to giggle helplessly.

"Paul wants to go and live in Millford," Fran said. "In one of those houses near the golf course. Do you want a bedroom of your own, decorated in your own choice of colours?"

"Do you want a bridesmaid?" Chris asked.

"I want two," Fran said chokily.

"You leave Florence Nightingale to me." Chris grinned. "She'll get used to the idea in time. I'll have to talk seriously to her! A few words of wisdom, you know!"

She got up. "Now go to sleep. I'll have to see that you get plenty of early nights from now on, so that you'll look radiant on your wedding day."

Fran laughed, and snuggled down in bed. But as Chris turned at the door, Fran spoke:

"I've been very worried about you, Chris, but it was silly of me not to realise what was wrong. I mean, my intuition should have told me — "

She stopped. "I've been too wrapped up in myself recently, I suppose."

"Yes, Mother," Chris said, her voice full of laughter. "That's the trouble with love, isn't it?" □

© *Betty Haworth 1979.*

MY VERY GOOD FRIEND
DRUMBUIE

By GIDEON SCOTT MAY

He started life as a small, vulnerable calf born into a Scottish blizzard. Before long, our friendship and loyalty to each other were as big and strong as my golden-haired Highlander himself . . .

THE storm crept in silently, like a wild cat stalking its prey, before suddenly revealing itself in a snarling, savage attack of swirling snowflakes. But, storm or no storm, it was calving time and the Highland cattle had to be checked.

I tramped through the carpet of white to where I knew they would be sheltering. The Thumb was a clearing in the woods where, Highland folklore has it, a giant, on the road to the isles, stumbled and fell, leaving his thumb print among the birch trees. It was a secluded spot where not even the most vicious storm could penetrate, but was forced to fly howling over the treetops.

Fighting my way through the white clouds of snow, I finally saw the cattle, steam rising from their nostrils, as they stood in a circle in the centre of The Thumb. I counted them quickly to find there was one missing. I peered through the swirling flakes and I saw her standing apart from the rest under a fir tree, its boughs weighed down, almost to breaking point, by the burden of snow.

It was Nighean Dhubh, the Black Maiden, a young heifer with a Gaelic pedigree as long as the dark, silken hair that rippled down her sides. She was near to calving and, like most young mothers, not at all sure of herself.

But where was she to go in this storm with the snow piled up high all around her? Already, just under her beautiful, black tail, there was a pair of legs with a little, pink nose in between them.

The heifer made an agitated half circle, gave a restless toss of her head and raised her long, dark eyelashes to reveal two deeply-disturbed eyes. They looked straight at me and I realised immediately that she was asking for help. Slipping up behind her, I gripped the tiny legs firmly as she took a step forward to leave the calf in my arms. The Maiden had given birth to a son!

For the time being, I kept mother and son within the confines of the croft buildings. The calf and I got to know and trust each other. He wasn't dark like his mother but a rich red with a colourful splash of golden hair cascading over his shoulders. I named him Drumbuie (golden back).

When the time came for the calves to be caught and experience

GIDEON'S WAY

70

the restrictions of the halter it became clear that Drumbuie's temperament was not the same as the others born that season. He didn't plunge and rear on his hind legs like they did before bowing to the inevitable. He just sniffed my bare arm and the rope in the friendliest fashion and never gave a quiver as the halter settled around his head. He then trotted happily by my side like a dog on a lead.

DRUMBUIE grew fast into a large and impressive member of the herd and made no secret of his love for my company. He would come forward to meet and greet me whenever I approached. He always got his reward — a tickle between his huge, hairy shoulder blades — which made him growl with pleasure.

Life through the summer months was peaceful once more for everyone and everything — until our neighbour's black Aberdeen-Angus bull literally bull-dozed his way through our stout, stone dyke.

I thought I would resolve things by picking up a stout stick and waving it in the face of the intruder, but the bull didn't take the slightest notice. Without a warning, he charged, butting me in the chest like a battering ram and sending me, spread-eagled and helpless, to the ground.

I choked over the hot steam from the bull's nostrils as he lowered his huge body to indulge in his speciality of kneeling on and crushing his victims. I could feel my ribs giving under the pressure of his big, bony knees and a red mist was floating in front of my eyes when I felt the ground shudder underneath me. It was Drumbuie, lifting the black bull from my body with his huge horns and throwing him to the ground on his back, with a resounding thump.

The black bull rose to his feet uncertainly and ran off, squealing with terror. Drumbuie followed him to the dyke and, with another scything sweep of his head gave him a helping horn over.

I crawled painfully towards Drumbuie, clawed my way up his side and clutched a handful of his golden mane. I then gave him the call that he had learned as a calf to come to the barn gate where his reward was a turnip, a carrot or cabbage, provided he "asked for it".

Drumbuie guided my stumbling steps to the gate and bawled, loud and long. Irralee heard him and, horrified at what she saw, gave Drumbuie his carrot and organised a trip to hospital for me to mend my broken ribs. □

Meeting with a Stranger

**This was a very special stranger —
the daughter of the man she loved.**

WE drove down from London early on Wednesday. It was a lovely morning, and Philip was beside me. I should have been happy, but I wasn't.

"All right, Laura?" He took his hand from the steering wheel for a moment, to cover mine as it lay in my lap.

"Yes, thank you." I shot him a swift smile, and looked back to the road ahead.

Caterford — 3 miles! Only a few minutes now. Just a few minutes and I would meet Suzy.

I found myself tensing inside, and wished I hadn't come. Perhaps it was wrong, descending on her like this. Perhaps another day would have been better, a day that was less important to her. After all, how could you be sure how a six-year-old would react?

But Philip had been determined. "I'm driving down on Wednesday. It's her Open Day at school. I promised."

I had understood. He loved his little daughter.

And I loved Philip, that was why I was here. One day soon Philip was going to ask me to marry him. I knew that. And I knew, too, that it all depended on Suzy.

She was Elaine's child — Elaine, his first love, who had married him when he was a struggling student, who had given him three brief years of happiness and a little daughter to remind him of her.

Now Philip loved me, wanted to marry me. And I wanted to marry him. But . . . *Caterford, 1 mile.* Almost there.

MEETING WITH A STRANGER

I tried to build up a picture of the child I was about to meet. Six years old . . . small for her age . . . loves cream cakes . . . afraid of spiders . . . adores babies . . .

That was all. The description might have fitted any small girl. Suddenly I realised Philip had told me almost nothing about her. I was about to meet a stranger.

But a stranger who was Elaine's child!

I had thought about it a lot, and I could accept that Philip had been happy before he had met me, that had been the moulding of the man I loved.

I didn't grudge Elaine her years of happiness, or resent Philip's memories of her.The past was the past. I could only feel an enormous sense of gratitude that I had come to be part of his present.

But Suzy was different. Suzy was not a gentle memory to be treasured in quiet moments, she was a living vital link with the past.

We had reached the outskirts of Caterford. I turned my head and watched Philip as he drove, seeing the strength of his face, the firm set of his mouth, and the muscles that could tighten stubbornly about his jaw.

He was strong, reliable, dependable. Life had not been all kind to him, but he had learned to come to terms with it without backing down. I admired him. I respected him. I loved him.

And, because I loved him, I understood him. I knew how easily he could be hurt, and how deeply. I could hurt him so much. That was why I had to be sure about Suzy.

I loved Philip, but that was not enough. Suzy was part of Philip, a deep, vulnerable part of him. I had to love Suzy, too, or it could never work.

"We go right through the town centre to the other side. A little bungalow. Aunt Bess has lived there about ten years, since Uncle Trevor died."

Aunt Bess, who'd so willingly taken Suzy when Elaine had died — one of the twin centres of Suzy's world. Daddy was the other one: Daddy, whose job took him all over the country, but who was a frequent, exciting visitor.

I glanced at Philip, and he smiled at me, a gentle, happy smile. Yet there was something in his eyes, his voice — tension, an anxiety. He so much wanted me to love Suzy.

Why shouldn't I?

I'd always loved children. When I had first started my training in the hospital, hadn't it been the children's ward I had enjoyed most? When I had been accepted for a special course, hadn't it been devoted to handicapped children? Yes, I loved children.

But Suzy was different. I didn't know how big I was, how capable of living face to face with a living memorial to Elaine in all the days to come.

For a moment I closed my eyes, and, slightly ashamed, silently prayed that Suzy was like Philip. At least just a little like Philip.

Aunt Bess was grey-haired, round and smiling. She met us in a flurry of happy confusion. Suzy usually had lunch at school, but today she was coming home.

I knew it was to give us a chance to meet before I was thrust upon her in the stiff atmosphere of a classroom. But Aunt Bess cheerfully made the excuse that she needed her costume for the class play, and it hadn't been finished until that morning.

"She's a daffodil," she explained, bustling us into the sitting-room. "And it's all made of crepe paper. She's so excited about it."

She patted Philip on the arm. "I promised you'd drive down and get her. There's not much time in the middle of the day and she won't want to be late back, not today. She'll be at the school gate."

She smiled. "Don't worry about Laura. She'll be all right with me."

AS the front door closed behind him, she hung my coat in the hall and called me through to the kitchen.

Aunt Bess was busy at the stove. I picked up a teacloth, and began to dry the oddments of china that stood draining beside the sink.

"Oh, my dear, you shouldn't!" She looked round smiling, then hesitated. "I'm glad you could come. Philip wrote and told me all about you." She nodded. "Yes, I'm so glad you could come today . . . to see Suzy."

"So am I." She was nice. I wanted to feel completely at ease with her, but I didn't. I wanted to ask her about Suzy, but I couldn't think where to begin. More, much more, I wanted to ask her about Elaine.

"It's very good of you to look after Suzy," I began hesitantly.

She shook her head. "Oh, she's a little darling, really." She chuckled. "Mind you, I'm not saying she's not tiring sometimes. Or perhaps I'm growing old."

I nodded. Philip had explained that. She had a sister who needed her company, a sister she loved. She would be sad to part with Suzy, of course, but she had done a good job for a long time.

"Aunt Bess." There seemed to be nothing else to call her, and my mind was more on the care with which I chose my words. "You knew Elaine, didn't you? I wondered . . . What was she like? I mean . . . Well, I don't want to ask Philip. I don't want to hurt him."

Aunt Bess nodded. Her eyes were understanding. "Yes, I knew her."

I looked away. "What was she like? I mean . . . What sort of a person was she?"

Aunt Bess pursed her lips. "She was lovely," she said honestly. "A gentle little soul, good and kind. Everybody loved her."

I nodded, thinking about Suzy . . . and wondering.

Gently, Aunt Bess took the teacloth from my hand. "Come along, now. Those things can wait. Philip and Suzy will only be a minute."

The tablecloth was spread and I was laying the cutlery when I heard the car.

"It's them!" Aunt Bess went running into the kitchen.

MEETING WITH A STRANGER

There was a clatter at the front door, Philip's voice, his laughter — and another voice, small, high-pitched, chattering excitedly.

Abruptly the door flew open, a tiny whirlwind in a navy checked pinafore went flying through and out the door into the kitchen. "My costume! Auntie Bess, my daffodil costume?"

Philip appeared in the doorway. "Suzy! Suzy! Come back!"

She came back obediently and stood in the kitchen doorway, a tiny girl with fair hair and a round face that was flushed with excitement. Bright blue eyes gazed at me from beneath a long fringe.

"Laura, this is Suzy," Philip was saying eagerly.

But I was staring at the child in front of me. She was nothing like Philip. Nothing at all. I searched her little face, the whole of her small, sturdy figure, but there was no trace of familiarity. I wanted to cry.

IT was a hurried lunch. Suzy talked most of the time. She was too excited to eat. One of her drawings had actually been hung on the wall, and we should be able to look at all her school books, and then, to cap it all, she would be a daffodil in the class play. It was all far too exciting for her to be bothered with food.

I watched across the table as first Aunt Bess, and then Philip, tried to tempt her with a mouthful or two. She was a fountain bubbling innocently with her own excitement, never dreaming for a moment how desperately important she was to me.

I watched Philip whisper to her, and point to the untouched food on her plate. And I saw her dart him a swift grin and plant a bold, confident kiss on his cheek.

Despite myself, I found I was noting every detail of her, every movement, every grimace, every gesture. Was that how Elaine had looked?

Was that the way she had tilted her head to one side, listening? Was that the way she had opened and closed her hands with impatient eagerness as she talked? The enthusiasm in her voice? Was that the way Elaine had talked, almost tripping over her words in the urgency of her thoughts?

"I mustn't be late! Oh, I mustn't be late!" Suddenly she was all concern. "Auntie Bess! My daffodil costume? You have sewn that green bit down, haven't you? The bit that kept sticking up and tickling my neck?

"Oh, and I must have a safety pin! Miss Travers said we must all have a safety pin, just in case."

I stood back as Aunt Bess bustled to despatch her. The safety pin was found. The daffodil costume was carefully laid in her arms. Gamely she struggled to balance the heap of green and yellow paper, and the tall golden trumpet head-dress.

"Are you sure you can manage?" Aunt Bess was doubtful.

"Perhaps — " Philip's voice was quiet. "Perhaps Laura could help you. How would it be if she carried it?"

Suzy considered me thoughtfully. "As long as you're careful," she agreed gravely. "You won't crumple it all up, will you? Promise?"

"I promise," I said seriously. Over her head I met Philip's eyes. He was smiling contentedly.

She sat beside me in the car, chattering happily and bobbing forward now and then to press her face against the window and wave excitedly.

"That's Tristan," she announced. "The boy we've just passed, with the blue shirt. He's very small, even smaller than me. And he has to wear glasses. He's a rabbit in the play."

She bobbed forward again. This time the wave was brief and half-hearted. "And that's Paul Carter. He's horrible. He hits people and makes them cry. He's the wolf in the play and nobody likes him, and it serves him right."

She was still talking as we turned in through the school gate. And I was still carrying the daffodil costume.

An elderly woman in crisp navy and white met us in the hall.

"Thank you." She relieved me of my burden and took Suzy's hand. "I'll take this to Miss Travers." She smiled at us. "The classrooms will be open to parents in a quarter of an hour. It's just to give the children a chance to settle. Meanwhile, perhaps you would like to have a look round and see the kind of work the classes are doing."

I glanced at Philip as Suzy was whisked away. His eyes followed her before they turned to me. "She's a chatterbox," he said, "but today she is very excited. I suppose it's understandable." He sounded apologetic.

ONE end of the hall was crowded with chairs, and at the other a dozen tables were spread with a display of handicrafts. There were rows of houses conjured up from cardboard boxes and paper and scraps of material. Matchboxes had been glued together into tiny chests of drawers. Egg-boxes, freshly striped with gaudy paint, had become bright lanterns.

And the centres of toilet rolls and masses of cotton wool had produced a flock of little white sheep, all huddled together and staring at us with bright button eyes.

Every item was labelled with a laboriously-printed name. Carefully, Philip searched among them. In the middle of the flock one sheep leaned against its neighbour. It was Suzy's. It had one short leg and its eyes were very close together. It looked depressed somehow, and very short sighted.

Philip laughed wryly, and leaned it back into place. "I don't think she's very good at this sort of thing," he said sadly.

The elderly woman in navy and white had rung a bell, and obediently the throng of parents had broken away into little trails headed for the various classrooms.

"But she has got a drawing hung on the wall, Philip. She said so."

The classroom was big and bright and Miss Travers, young and flushed, stood smiling before the blackboard.

Suzy pounced upon us the moment we stepped through the door, and hauled us to the array of drawings that adorned the back wall.

"There!" She pointed with enormous pride. "That's mine. It's a day in the country. The cows are a bit thin and that tree looks as if it's falling over, but Miss Travers says it's the best I've ever done."

"It's very good," Philip said, and looked at me hopefully.

I nodded quickly. "It's very good indeed," I said. But Suzy was tugging at my sleeve. Obediently I leant down.

"That's Tristan," Suzy whispered. "The one in the blue shirt with glasses. You remember? His mummy can't come today because she's sick, and I think he's a bit sad. So perhaps you'd better have a look at his picture as well."

I glanced at Philip, then at the forlorn little figure sitting alone at his desk. But Suzy was already charging across the classroom.

"Come on, Tristan. They want to see your picture, too." She brought him over, hauling him by the hand. "He's a rabbit, aren't you, Tristan?" She beamed encouragingly at him. "His mummy is sick but his gran made him a lovely costume."

Tristan smiled at us shyly, his pale cheeks warming at our interest. "It's got two big ears," he ventured. "And there's wire in them so they won't fall down. My grandad helped with that."

Suzy sighed contentedly. "Show them your picture, Tristan," she said briskly. She smiled at Philip. "Then you have to look at my books. And I suppose you'd better have a look at Tristan's as well."

We looked at Tristan's first, then at Suzy's. Tristan's were clean and tidy and stacked in a neat little pile on his desk. Suzy's were dog-eared, and there were blue crosses against most of her sums.

She watched as Philip silently flicked over the pages, then she smiled innocently up into his face. "I can't do sums," she said happily. "But I can read. Last week I read a whole page to Miss Travers. I could read to you now, except I've lost my book."

Philip patted her head and smiled, but he didn't say anything. I loved him for not showing his disappointment. He was the man I loved, but he was also a proud father. He had wanted so much to show Suzy off, to see that she made a good impression on me.

Suddenly the parents were all dutifully filing back into the hall. Suzy accompanied us as far as the classroom door.

"Remember, a daffodil," she insisted. "You'll know it's me because I'm the little one on the end. And you will clap, won't you?"

We promised, and I followed Philip into the hall, and sat beside him in one of the neat rows. The tables had been cleared, the piano had been pushed forward. The entertainment was about to begin.

There was a long noisy silence. Teachers tiptoed to and fro. Doors opened and closed abruptly. Muffled children's voices rose to a soft babble, then were silenced. The parents murmured awkwardly amongst themselves.

I glanced sideways at Philip.

His eyes were serious as they met mine. "Are you sorry you came?" he asked softly.

I shook my head. I was unhappy, but I wasn't sorry. It had been important to come. It had been important to find out.

The elderly woman in navy and white was in the middle of the floor, smiling and explaining. There would be songs and dances and even a percussion band. But first Miss Travers' class would perform a little play.

I heard, but I was not listening. I was still looking at Philip. I wondered what he would say if I told him the thoughts that were racing round my mind. *She's not like you, Philip. I've watched her. I've listened to her. But there's nothing about her that reminds me of you.*

But he was gazing ahead, listening attentively.

A ND now I will hand you over to Miss Travers." The elderly woman waved an introductory hand, smiled, then, glancing round, she settled into the empty chair beside me.

Miss Travers came through the arch that led from the corridor into the hall. Behind her there was a flurry of multi-coloured crepe paper, and small faces peeped and giggled.

"Our play is called 'A Day In Spring'. " Her cheeks were very pink, and she looked harassed. "We hope you enjoy it." She glanced back, whispered sternly, then went to the piano and began to play.

All eyes went to the arch, where a small girl with blonde curls came hesitantly forward.

"It is spring," she began. "It is a lovely day in spring." She smiled carefully and waved a hand. "See, the sun has just come out."

A large yellow cardboard sun popped eagerly out from behind the arch. A small boy grinned happily over the top of it as it bounced across to settle beside the piano.

Miss Travers played on.

The little girl with the blonde curls waved her hand stiffly again. "And the yellow daffodils are all dancing in the wind."

Beside me Philip suddenly leaned forward. He loved his daughter so much.

With the rest I stared at the arch. Four little girls, all dressed in daffodil costumes skipped eagerly into the middle of the hall and posed for their dance. There was no sign of Suzy.

Miss Travers faltered at the piano as every eye went back to the arch. From somewhere beyond it there was the whisper of voices. It grew louder.

MEETING WITH A STRANGER

So did Miss Travers' music. From her vantage point it was obvious she could see into the corridor, and she was frowning.

The little blonde girl fidgeted, shuffled her feet, then anxiously began afresh. "It is spring. It is a lovely day in spring . . ."

The voices beyond the arch rose aggressively. There was the unmistakable sound of a scuffle.

I looked at Philip. A pink flush was creeping up his cheeks.

The music stopped, and Miss Travers rose to her feet. For a moment it was as though in her agitation she had forgotten the assembly of wide-eyed parents.

"Suzy!" she called. "Suzy!"

There was a moment's silence, then Suzy appeared. The ring of yellow paper petals about her neck dropped, one was torn and flapping, and the trumpet headdress was bent. But she was smiling.

She beamed towards the piano. "It's all right, Miss Travers," she said happily. "Paul Carter bent Tristan's ears down, then laughed at him because he looked silly. But I made him bend them back. Everything's all right now."

She smiled contentedly round the hall, then skipped forward and took her place beside the other daffodils.

A ripple of amusement ran through the audience, then was politely stifled. Philip's cheeks were scarlet. He looked unhappy and embarrassed. I wanted to comfort him, but I could not resist staring back at the tiny daffodil on the end of the row.

Crumpled, bedraggled and with her golden trumpet leaning pathetically, she was the picture of innocent anticipation as, toe pointed, arms outstretched, she waited for Miss Travers to restart the music.

The elderly woman in navy and white, sitting beside me, sighed.

"That's our Suzy," she said resignedly, but her eyes were dancing with amusement. "She has the heart of an angel, the innocence of a cherub, and an infinite capacity for causing chaos." She chuckled. "But that's Suzy. There's no-one quite like Suzy."

I stared from her amused face back to the daffodils. They were dancing to the music, eagerly, enthusiastically, especially the smallest one at the end.

There's no-one quite like Suzy. The words rang through my mind.

It was true. Of course it was true. I had been so stupid, swayed by my own apprehensions, blinded by my own fears.

Suzy wasn't another Philip any more than she was another Elaine. She wasn't a replica of anyone.

She was herself, a glorious, robust little human being waiting for time, and love, and the whole exciting adventure of living to mould her into a wonderful person.

I glanced at Philip. He still looked unhappy, and I still wanted to comfort him, but it wasn't the time or the place.

Later, when we were alone, I could tell him what he wanted so much to hear. But for the moment I just wanted to watch the little daffodil on the end . . . the one that one day soon was going to be mine. □

Little Donkey...

This little Spanish donkey is looking longingly over the fence for a new home — why not take him into yours?

Materials Required — Of Littlewoods Double Knit 100% Courtelle, 1 x 100 gram ball in natural or chocolate brown, also available in 25 gram mini balls, small amounts of pink and black yarn; several pieces of different-coloured felt; braid; one pair of 3¼ mm (No. 10) knitting needles.

For best results it is essential to use the recommended yarn. If you have difficulty in obtaining the yarn, write direct, enclosing a stamped addressed envelope to the following address for stockists:

Andrea Wood, Department 28, Littlewoods Chainstores Ltd., Albert Dock, Liverpool L70 1AD (Tel. 051-2426114).

Measurements — Height, 31 centimetres, *12¼ inches,* approximately.
Tension — 24 stitches and 32 rows to 10 centimetres, *4 inches,* measured over stocking-stitch using 3¼ mm needles.

Abbreviations — K — knit; P — purl; st.(s) — stitch(es); st.-st. — stocking- stitch; cm — centimetres; ins — inches.

BODY (Make 1)

Cast on 40 sts. and work 22 cm, 8¾ ins, in st.-st., ending with a purl row.

Cast off.

LEGS (Make 4)

With black, cast on 26 sts. and work 3 cm, 1¼ ins, in st.-st., ending with a purl row.

Break off black, join in brown and work 11 cm, 4¼ ins, in st.-st., ending with a purl row.

Cast off.

HEAD (Left Side)

Cast on 22 sts. and work 2 rows in st.-st. Decrease 1 st. at beginning and increase 1 st. at end of next and following 3 alternate rows. Purl one row.

Next row — Decrease 1 st. at beginning, knit to end.

Cast on 11 sts. at beginning of next row — 32 sts.

Work straight until work measures 9 cm, 3½ ins, ending with a purl row.

Decrease 1 st. at beginning of next row and at same edge on next 5 rows.

Cast off.

Work right side to match, reversing shaping.

EARS (Make 2)

Cast on 11 sts. and work 22 rows in st.-st.

Decrease 1 st. at each end of next and following 4th row, then following 3rd row and following alternate row — 3 sts.

Cast off.

NOSE (Make 2)

With pink, cast on 22 sts. and work 4 rows in st.-st.

Decrease 1 st. at each end of next and following 4th row; then following 3rd row and every alternate row until 10 sts. remain. Cast off.

TAIL (Make 1)

Cast on 21 sts. and work 4 rows in st.-st. Cast off.

★ ★ ★ ★ ★ ★ ★ ★ ★

TO MAKE UP

Fold body in half and join cast-on and cast-off edges. Join one end and stuff. Join remaining seam.

Join head seams, leaving front open. Stuff head.

Sew straight edges of nose to head, leaving a small opening, stuff nose and join seam. Sew head to body.

Join long seam of legs and base, stuff and join remaining seam then sew to body at four corners.

Roll tail with purl side out and join seam. Make a tassel from pink yarn and sew to end of tail, then sew to body.

Cut lengths of black and knot to head to form mane.

Cut out same shape as ears from pink felt, sew together and sew to head.

Cut out eye, nostril and mouth shapes from felt and sew to nose and head.

Cut out a saddle shape (an elongated oval) from felt and sew on braid as illustrated in photograph.

Cut a strip of felt to fit under donkey to saddle. Sew this strip to saddle then put it on donkey. □

The medallion was precious to her — to both of them — but it was still a chain, holding her prisoner . . .

In Every Link
A Memory

M AY Turner arrived home that evening feeling sad, empty and tired. She had had a hectic week; the last hectic week she would ever have.

There had been the presentation from Saint Jude's for thirty years' unstinting devotion to the hospital. There had been all the business of retiring, shaking the hand of everyone from the under-gardener to the senior consultant. And lastly there had been the awful temptation — to give in to Giles at last.

"May, there's no excuse any more," he'd pleaded. "There's no-one to consider but yourself — or me — any longer. You're fifty-five. Still young enough to enjoy a good marriage with me. I've been waiting ten years now, and I still love you!"

IN EVERY LINK A MEMORY

She had smiled to take the sting from her reply. "I don't love you, Giles."

"Yes, you do."

The flat contradiction had taken her aback. She had stopped smiling and a small flush had stained her cheeks.

"You must give me credit for knowing my own feelings, Giles."

"I'm sorry, May, I can't. You've not thought about your own feelings for so long that you don't know them any more."

"I assure you — "

"If I went away — threw up my job — disappeared from your life, then you'd realise that you love me. Maybe I should do that."

"Don't be absurd, my dear. You're too good an administrator — "

The argument had carried on till it had almost become a row. And all the time she had been so tempted to take his hand and let the companionship they had shared at work continue into her personal life. Except that it wouldn't be fair to Giles.

He had been married before and had a grown-up family. He knew what it was like to love one woman and one woman only. He couldn't accept that May Turner's emotions were different. Her "devotion" had always been to scores of people, not just one.

She put her hand over her eyes momentarily. Perhaps that was why she had been such a good matron of Saint Jude's, because she was incapable of intense personal love.

May sat down wearily. Soon she would make her evening meal as usual. Then she would go for a brisk walk through the dark wintry village and then home to a play on television and an early night.

She was getting a well-deserved rest, the senior consultant of the hospital had told her. And that's what it was. Not the time to be starting a new life — especially one as young-hearted as marriage. After all, she was fifty-five. She had earned a well-deserved rest.

Besides, she was very set in her ways, and determined to stay that way. It was the only way to hang on to the self-discipline that had kept her . . . safe. As a good nurse, she'd had to be caring, but detached. How could she change now, and give her love to one man?

Her thoughts were interrupted by a knock at the back door. She got up to see her next-door-neighbour waving a small parcel happily.

"Hello, Miss Turner," she said as soon as May opened the door. "I expect you're feeling a bit sad today. This should cheer you up though. It's come all the way from Australia!" She placed the parcel in May's hands and left with a cheery smile.

Confused, May turned the parcel over in her hands. Australia? She didn't know anyone in Australia.

She took it inside and tore at the thick padded wrapping. There was an envelope, officially stamped, and a long box. She opened the lid of the box and there, nestling on tissue, was a Saint Christopher medallion on a gold chain.

May gaped in surprise. As she stared at the medallion, her eyes misted over and the years seemed to fall away, so many years . . .

Seventeen-year-old May had been thrilled when Grace asked her to be a bridesmaid at her wedding to Steven, who was in the forces.

"It's going to be a modest wedding," Grace warned, in case May's excitement ran away with her. "Afternoon dresses — we'll go mad with our hats, of course. As Steven is going out to Korea next week, I don't feel a white wedding — "

"Of course not," May breathed adoringly.

Whatever Grace said or did was perfect with her. Grace was five years older than May, and she'd lived next door to her all their lives. She'd wheeled May in her pushchair, taught her to play hop-scotch and to skip and to wave her hair with hot curling tongs.

She was a nurse, so of course May was going to be a nurse, too. They might meet out in the Far East, if only the war would last another year till May was eighteen.

G RACE smiled happily. "Harry Malleson, Steven's best friend, is going to be best man. After the actual service he drops behind and escorts you into the vestry — "

"And then we walk down the aisle together after." May was already well schooled in such matters. "Is he nice? Is he dark or fair? Do I call him Harry or Mr Malleson — ?"

"Captain Malleson." Grace looked a little regretful. "He's gorgeous-looking, actually. But too old for you, May. And he's engaged to someone in Yorkshire. Sorry."

"Don't be silly. I don't mind. It's just that it's all so wonderful and romantic. You and Steven — "

"Getting married in a hurry at the beginning of a war when we might not see each other again for weeks," Grace interrupted drily. And then, her hands gripping together, "Maybe never . . ."

"Oh, Grace . . ." The two girls clung together, suddenly frightened of the future.

The following day Steven gave May a tiny gold Saint Christopher on a chain.

"It's the most beautiful thing I've ever seen, Steven," she said softly. "You should have given it to Grace."

"This is what I'm giving to Grace." He showed her the wedding ring in its box. Their initials were engraved along the inside.

May felt her eyes watering. She couldn't wait to fall in love and be loved by someone.

"Cheer up, May." Steven nudged her. "You're not losing Grace, remember, you're gaining me!" She laughed obediently and let him fasten the chain around her neck.

And then there was a knock at the door and her mother showed "Steven's friend" into the sitting-room.

Steven shook his hand warmly. "You introduced yourself to Mrs Turner?" He smiled at May's mother. "She has made the cake and loaned her daughter for the occasion."

His smile included May. "This is my best man, May. Harry Malleson. Harry — this is Grace's bridesmaid, May."

At first May wondered why Grace had described him as "gorgeous-

IN EVERY LINK A MEMORY

"If I disappeared from your life then you'd realise you loved me."

looking." His hair was mid-brown and matched his eyes. His nose was rather too long and his jaw line much pronounced for traditional good looks. But she had to admit there was something about him. Something warm and friendly. As if he was having a good time in a quiet sort of way and it was all because of you.

He was to sleep for two nights in their spare room. The first evening they all went out for a meal, the parents and the young people together. Nine of them; sitting around a table in the town's best restaurant, with a string quartet of elderly men playing Viennese waltzes.

"Can you manage the old-fashioned waltz, May?" Harry asked.

Grace and Steven were already pirouetting expertly among the few dancers on the floor.

"We've done it at school." May felt herself blushing for some unknown reason. "But I'm always the gentleman. I don't know whether I could be a lady."

They all laughed and her father spoke to her fondly. "May, you couldn't be anything but a lady even if you tried."

May blushed harder than ever.

"Come on," Harry prompted. "Let's try. I'm hopeless, but if you can push me around a bit — "

He chose the darkest part of the floor and they stumbled around hopelessly. Then he whispered in her ear, "Come closer, May. Stand on my feet — of course you won't hurt me — when did May blossom ever weigh anything? That's it. Now let's see what we can do."

Hiding her face in his shoulder, she clung to him helplessly as they moved out into the dancing spotlight. They twirled past their table where the parents clapped, surprised at their expertise, reversed in front of the violinists and swept back to the safety of the dusty palms just as the final chord vibrated to its close.

They applauded, and she couldn't take her eyes from his.

"You're marvellous, May. Will you give me some of those lessons you have at school?"

She gasped and giggled. "Oh, Harry — stop making fun of me!"

He took her hand and led her into the formation for the valeta. "I'm not making fun of you, May blossom. Honestly, I've never danced like that before in my life."

IN EVERY LINK A MEMORY

*"You must give
me credit for
knowing my
feelings."*

"I should hope not. I expect your other partners can manage for themselves!"

"Exactly!" He turned her under his arm and held her close. "They manage perfectly for themselves and by themselves. I have never danced with someone and felt like one person instead of two."

She still did not know whether he was teasing or not. It made no difference. She was already in love with him.

HE looked splendid at the wedding in his dress uniform. When Grace handed back her flowers he turned and watched and smiled. After he had passed over the ring, he dropped back and stood by her and tucked her hand in his arm when they walked into the vestry.

And as the strains of "The Wedding March" rang through the half-empty church she walked proudly behind Grace and tried to imagine that she and Harry . . . she and Harry . . .

He took her out for a meal alone that evening. Grace and Steven were spending two nights in North Wales and the parents were too tired to go out again.

She tried to speak lightly. "I wonder whether I'll ever see you again? Maybe we'll meet up in ten years and you won't recognise me."

"If we didn't meet for forty years, I'd know you, May. In a bath-chair — white and wrinkled — "

She pinched his arm playfully. "In forty years' time, I'll be fifty seven. My Aunt Esme's fifty-five and she wears make-up and goes off to the pictures."

He frowned hard, pretending to consider the matter. "I think I'd prefer you not to fight the advancing years. Grow old gracefully, that sort of thing."

She felt suddenly saddened. "I wish you'd take me seriously, Harry. I asked you a serious question."

He reached for her hand. "I took it seriously, May. What I meant was; even when you're an old lady, to me you will still be as you are now."

"A little girl," she said resentfully.

"Half child, half woman," he corrected her, his voice very gentle.

She gripped his hand, feeling as if she was drowning. "Harry — couldn't you wait until I'm a whole woman?"

He didn't smile. His eyes, soft as brown velvet, were unreadable. "I'm engaged, May. To a lovely girl I've known all my life."

She felt ashamed. "I'm sorry," she whispered. "Sorry . . ."

"Don't be. Never be sorry for courage, May. And it takes courage to reach for happiness."

She shook her head despairingly. "If anything should change . . . in the future . . ."

With his free hand, he touched her hair. "Then that would be a different matter, wouldn't it? I should have to take my courage in both hands and come here to see what had happened to you in the meantime."

She couldn't see him any more for the tears in her eyes.

The next morning she went to see him on to the train. He leaned out of the window and took the sandwiches her mother had cut for him and kissed her lightly on the cheek.

"I'll never forget you, May. Whatever happens I'll always remember these two days and the May blossom that bloomed in the autumn."

On a sudden impulse, she reached behind her neck and unclasped the gold Saint Christopher that Steven had given her.

"Keep this — please, Harry. Not as a souvenir of me or anything silly. Just to keep you safe. Please."

He took it reluctantly. "All right — "

The train began to move. "Whatever happens — keep it!" she called. "Keep it till the day you die!"

The war finished before Grace could get her posting. Steven was killed and Grace became very thin and worked much too hard.

By the time May had finished her nurse's training she heard that Harry was married. She had met other men who told her they were in love with her. She smiled and looked after them with dedication. When they left there was always someone else demanding her time and attention.

When Grace went to London to make a new life for herself, May was already convinced that her way was best. Love was more effective and far safer when it was objective and given to all who needed it.

She joined the staff of Saint Jude's when she was twenty-five and ten years later became the youngest matron the hospital had ever had. And there she had stayed until her retirement today, at fifty-five. And she'd never given a thought to young May Turner, nor to Captain Harry Malleson . . .

NOW, May fingered the Saint Christopher she hadn't seen for thirty-eight years. She held it against the light and wept a little for the girl she had been and the people that girl had known and loved. "Keep it till the day you die," she had said.

With trembling hands she opened the envelope that accompanied the medallion. The letter was from a firm of solicitors in Sydney. It was short and formal.

Dear Miss Turner,

We regret to inform you that Mr Harold Malleson died here on November 24, 1978, aged 68. In accordance with his expressed wishes, we are sending you the enclosed medallion.

So he *had* kept it until he died. He had remembered, even from so far away. He couldn't change his life, but he had remembered.

May felt a small ache in the centre of her being. It had been nothing, of course. He'd been nearly thirty and she a schoolgirl and they had known each other for just two days.

And yet . . . had she honestly waited for him all these years and hoped that one day he could come back? Of course not. It was ridiculous.

She had to be honest. Before today, and this parcel, she'd probably have just thought of him as one more man who had gone away from her and probably never thought of her again. Like all the patients who had professed "undying love," confusing it with gratitude.

After all, Harry Malleson had said nothing — promised nothing. All she'd ever really hoped was that he'd live a full and happy life, and that the medallion would protect him. And perhaps it had . . .

May looked slowly round her neat home. Yes. She herself had had a very full and a very happy life since she had met Harry Malleson. So full and happy that she had hardly spared him a thought.

Yet . . . she had never forgotten him, not quite. And — she pressed the medallion against her face — he had never forgotten her.

So she did know what it was like to be in love. And to be loved in return. There was no safety, no security in it. She took a deep breath, remembering what Giles had said. "You've not thought about your own feelings for so long that you don't know them any more."

Was he right? She tried to imagine him carrying out his threat to throw up his job and go away. She had seen it as the loss of a good hospital administrator. But what would it mean to her, personally?

She closed her eyes suddenly, pressing the Saint Christopher hard on her cheek until it hurt. She couldn't face that again. To love someone and to lose him . . . not again.

She opened her eyes and walked slowly to the mirror above the mantelpiece. Her eyes watched her reflection as she clasped the chain around her still slender neck.

She spoke aloud, "Yes. You would still recognise me, Harry. I haven't changed much outside. And inside I'm just the same."

She smiled and went to the telephone. Giles' number was familiar to her but her fingers trembled a little as she picked out the digits.

When he answered she spoke tremulously. "Giles, I've been thinking about what you said. Leaving the hospital — leaving the town — "

There was a pause. "Yes?"

She was blinded by tears. "Don't," she whispered. "Please don't, Giles." □

Susan In-The-Middle

On one side was the woman who had loved and cared for her. On the other side — her mother.

IT was the loneliness that sent me back to my home town. I had never been alone before. Not totally alone. Aunt Jessie's birthday card was my last precious link with our past, and I couldn't stop thinking about a woman I hadn't seen in years, since I was a little girl.

A month after my mother's funeral I gave up my secretarial job. I didn't think clearly what I was doing. I just wanted to go back home. I just wanted to see *her* again.

I arrived early one morning, booked into a hotel and an hour later I was picking my way across the town.

Nine years is a long time, and I was still only nineteen. Much had changed, much I couldn't remember. But it didn't matter. I knew where I was going.

It took me twenty minutes. Out of the town centre, into the forest of old houses that surrounds it. Gradually it all became familiar. Childish memories came racing back. At last, the little shop where I had bought ice-cream, the park where I had played.

Then suddenly I was there. Fiveacre Road! The sign was grubby and peeling. A square, grey block of flats had sprung up where I remembered only a vast, deserted patch of grass, dotted with dandelions. But beyond I could see the old houses.

It was at that moment that doubt struck me, like a black cloud looming suddenly across a clear blue sky.

Up till then it had seemed so simple. I had wanted to see her. I had wanted to talk to her. I had wanted just to be with her. Now reality had reared up before me, and it wasn't simple any more.

I was being stupid. Stupid and unfeeling. Why should she want to see me again? Surely the sight of me could only open up old wounds, bring her more unhappiness?

I stood alone at the corner of the street, and I told myself I was being ridiculous. It was all in the past. People forgot. They went on living their lives. Houses changed hands. Neighbours moved away. Perhaps she, too, had moved away.

I started forward at that. I am not sure why except that the thought twisted miserably inside me. I didn't want her to be there. I wanted everything to be as it had once been.

I stared across at No. 37 but there was no sign of her. Just the house, the same as ever and painfully familiar. And the garden, different yet strangely the same. A few shrubs grown large and sprawling, and beside the gate the lavender bush we had bought and planted together.

Miserably I walked on. But at the end of the street I stopped. I had to turn back. It would be possible to cut across the back streets and avoid Fiveacre Road but I knew I couldn't.

I would walk slowly back, and stop just a moment to stare at the old house, then I would go away. That was the best plan. I had never done her any harm, yet how could I bring her anything but unhappiness? And, surely, she had suffered enough.

I was absorbed with my thoughts. I came suddenly again to the garden of No. 37. And there he was! A man with greying hair in a sagging yellow pullover and a pair of old trousers, his arms full of gardening tools.

He stared at me curiously as I stood gaping at him.

Heat flushed my cheeks. For a moment I could neither think nor move, then, "You live here?" The question came instinctively.

He nodded, obviously surprised. "Yes."

"But . . . I thought . . ." He was staring at me. I didn't know how to go on.

He glanced round uncertainly, then, as though suddenly understanding, he smiled. "Oh, I see! The garden? You thought perhaps the house was empty? Oh, no. My wife and I don't usually keep it like this, but she's been ill, you see, and it has run rather wild . . ."

I wasn't listening. I was thinking of her. She wasn't here any more. "I see. Thank you," I said quickly. Then I hurried on down the street.

I walked blindly, heading nowhere in particular, and found myself at the park. Miserably I wandered in and sat on a swing.

"It's all in the past," I told myself. The best thing you can do is go away and forget.

But I knew I couldn't forget. I could remember it all too clearly, right back to the first time I met her . . . over the garden wall.

WE had just moved in next door, my mother and I. Two little rooms upstairs at the back, a tiny bedroom and a living-room that looked out over the garden. I was nine years old, and for over an hour I had sat gazing out the window while the boxes and suitcases were unpacked and the familiar possessions were pushed away into unfamiliar cupboards and drawers.

I was used to the pattern. We had moved many times, my mother and I, and I knew from experience how irritable and edgy she could be at times like this. I wasn't afraid of her. When she was happy she was fun. But that was only sometimes. Other times I tried my best to be quiet and obedient.

But the garden beckoned irresistibly. A bright little world of paths and flowerbeds and green grass and vegetables in straight neat rows. I had lived only in flats that were two, sometimes three, floors up. I had looked out only on grey concrete yards and busy streets. I wanted more than anything to get into that garden, and when my mother went into the bedroom . . .

The house was quiet. Even the latch on the back door made not a sound. I thought no-one had seen or heard. I can still remember the sunlight and the grass crisp beneath my feet, and the birds flying up ahead of me as I walked.

I had almost reached the vegetables when the window slammed up. Mrs Jarvis lived on the ground floor, and her voice was loud and harsh. "No! Not in the garden! You're not allowed in the garden!"

I burst into tears. Surprise perhaps. Or guilt. My mother would be angry, and nothing was fun when she was angry.

"Oh dear." I heard a soft voice. It was a moment before I realised where it had come from. Then I saw her face over the wall of the garden next door. I don't remember noticing anything except that her eyes were blue and kind and she smiled. "Don't cry. Please. Don't cry."

"I didn't mean to scare her." Mrs Jarvis had come out into the garden. To me she looked big and ugly and frightening, but there was concern in her voice. "It's just that . . . Well, you know what my old man is about his garden. He'd blow his top if she touched any of his flowers."

"I was only looking." I couldn't stop the tears, and I had no handkerchief. I wiped them away with the back of my hand and more came.

SUSAN-IN-THE-MIDDLE

"Moved into my rooms today. Just her and her mother." Mrs Jarvis's voice was almost kind. "I didn't mean to upset her. It's just that . . ."

"Won't you stop crying and tell me your name?" It was the soft voice again.

"Susan." I barely whispered it.

"Well, Susan, you could come and play in my garden." She was smiling at me. "If your mother didn't mind, of course."

"I'll tell her, Mrs Tempson." Mrs Jarvis was not one to hesitate. She picked me up in her arms and dumped me over the wall. "She won't mind. Give her a chance to get settled in peace."

To me at that moment hers was a dream garden, the kind children wandered through in the books my mother read to me when she was happy. Bright flowers everywhere, even a little pool and a tiny waterfall.

I remember I just stood where I had been unceremoniously dumped, the tears drying on my cheeks, but afraid to move.

"Come on, Susan." She slipped her hand into mine. It was soft and warm and somehow it felt good and reassuring. "I think you and I are going to be friends."

AND she was right. It wasn't long before we were spending hours together.

"She's a fine person, is Mrs Tempson." I had heard Mrs Jarvis assure my mother. "Loves children but I've heard she can't have any of her own. The little girl will be all right with her."

And my mother had been content. Almost she had seemed grateful to ring the next-door bell and hand me over when she brought me home from school. I understood. She was busy. Mothers were often busy. And then they were tired.

It didn't matter. I had a whole wonderful garden to explore and someone to talk to whenever I felt like it. Aunt Jessie always seemed happy to listen.

It was her idea I should call her Aunt Jessie. No-one ever had before and it seemed to make her sad and happy at the same time.

Mr Tempson was nice to me, too. I wasn't used to men. Other children at school had fathers but no-one had even mentioned mine. At first I felt tongue-tied and ill-at-ease as he towered, smiling, over me. But then he took to squatting down to chat to me, and gradually I began to smile at him too and call him Uncle Edward.

It was Aunt Jessie who first told me about the job Uncle Edward had found for my mother, as his secretary.

"She's going to work in his office," she explained happily. "She'll drop you at school on her way in the mornings and then I'll be waiting when you come out. We can go to the park, or to the shops, or just come back here and have tea together. You'd like that, wouldn't you, Susan?"

Of course I liked it. I couldn't imagine why I shouldn't have. I loved being with Aunt Jessie.

It was a wonderful summer. I didn't see Mother so much but when I did she seemed different somehow. She didn't seem to get cross so quickly, even when I broke things.

And she began to look prettier, a lot prettier, even though she had to work hard, sometimes till late into the evenings.

Then I would stay on with Aunt Jessie, and she would let me help her cook supper and lay the table. She even made me a little check apron with a pocket for my handkerchief.

And when autumn came and the garden was grey and chilly she would light the fire and we would both curl up on the hearthrug and she would tell me stories while we waited for my mother and Uncle Edward. She knew endless stories. It was as though she had been saving them up, waiting for me.

Gradually my mother seemed to work late more and more. Often I only saw her when she chased me quickly to bed, or when she hurried me through my breakfast.

At first I cared, but gradually it didn't seem to matter. I had Aunt Jessie. When I got a gold star at school for my writing or my sums I couldn't wait to tell her. And when I proudly carried back a precious drawing or a plaited paper basket or a daisy fashioned from cartons, it was Aunt Jessie who treasured it, and found a special place for it on the sideboard.

MY birthday is in the middle of October. "I'll make you a cake with pink icing," she promised one evening.

"And ten candles," I begged. "And you'll all help me to blow them out, you and Mother and Uncle Edward."

I remember how she hesitated, staring into the fire. I had never seen her look unhappy before and I was concerned. But she tousled my hair and laughed and only her eyes were sad as she promised I could have my candles.

That evening we waited for Mother and Uncle Edward to come home, and at last I fell asleep on the rug in front of the fire. When I woke I was sleeping in Aunt Jessie's little spare room with a night-light burning beside me, and somewhere in the house someone was shouting and someone else was crying.

It was Aunt Jessie who answered my call. She blew out the night-light before I could see her face, and told me I was really too big to need it.

Then she held my hand in the darkness, and I could feel her fingers trembling. I wanted to ask her what was wrong, why she was

G

unhappy, but after a minute she covered me up and kissed me. Then she handed me my birthday card. But why so early?

Next morning Uncle Edward took me home, and already my mother had begun to pack.

I was almost ten years old. Four more days and I would have had my pink-iced cake with its bright candles. Instead my mother was packing, her face white, her eyes red-rimmed. All the familiar things were coming out of the cupboards and drawers and being crammed into the old boxes and suitcases. And I didn't understand.

I didn't understand what was happening, or why. I didn't know where we were going, or for how long. I didn't know why Mrs Jarvis scowled at my mother and passed me by in tight-lipped silence. I didn't know why I wasn't going to school.

And I didn't know why I couldn't go in and see Aunt Jessie.

My mother told me as I sat silently in the bare living-room, watching her as she reddened her lips and hastily ran a comb through her long blonde hair.

"We're going away, Susan. Things have changed. We're going away, and . . . Uncle Edward is coming with us."

"And Aunt Jessie?" She was my first thought.

"No." I remember my mother didn't look at me. Her voice sounded strange and choked. "Just Uncle Edward."

I remember driving off that morning in Uncle Edward's car. Aunt Jessie was standing at the window watching as the suitcases were carried out and stacked into the boot, and I was bundled into the back seat.

I had never seen her look so unhappy. I had never seen anyone ever look so unhappy as she looked. I knelt up on the seat to wave to her, waving and waving until all I could see was the gate and the lavender bush beside it. Then I cried and cried.

AT that memory the tears started instinctively to my eyes. Impatiently I brushed them away.

That was nine years ago. Nine long years during which I had never forgotten her. Always secretly I had cherished a dream that one day I would come back and find her.

But now she was gone. Strangers lived in the house she had loved. Strangers worked in the garden she had cherished. And I had no idea where she was. I would never be able to find her again.

Never . . . unless . . .

I didn't stop to reason. Only one thought filled my mind. If I didn't find her now I would never see her again. Someone must know where she had gone, surely?

I half walked, half ran. I was thinking only of myself. What would I tell her if I found her? Would she be happier, knowing? Knowing that it had all gone sour? That the man she had loved had stayed with us only three years? That my mother had never stopped regretting.

I didn't know. I only knew I had to try to find her.

The man was still in the garden. The sleeves of his old yellow pullover were rolled up, now and he had a pair of secateurs in his hands.

"Excuse me . . ."

He looked up, surprised at first, then smiling, and came across to me at the gate.

"I'm sorry to bother you, but . . ." I was out of breath. I tried to gather myself. "There was a lady lived here before. A Mrs Tempson. Do you know where she went?"

He stared at me blankly. My heart sank and, in my anxiety, words sprang to my lips. "I want to find her. If you have any idea . . . it's . . . very important. I used to know her . . . a long time ago . . ."

He was still staring at me, surprise mixed with curiosity. "Well . . . I think you'd better come through and see my wife . . . She's in the garden."

I hesitated. I didn't want to step back into that garden so full of memories. But, more than anything, I wanted to find her, and he was holding the gate open for me . . .

I walked behind him round the side of the house. The tiny rosebush I had watched her plant had grown and covered the arch that led to the back garden. He stood back for me to pass.

I don't know what I expected. Perhaps a neglected tangle like the front garden. But in the centre the weeds and the overgrown bushes had been pushed back. The pool and the tiny waterfall were just as I remembered, and beside them, on the little clearing of newly-mown grass, stood two brightly-striped chairs.

In one of them sat Aunt Jessie, a little older, a little plumper, but unmistakable. She was smiling.

I stopped in surprise. I had always remembered her sad and lonely. Perhaps, without realising, I had hoped we could console each other. But she was happy. She had forgotten.

I would have turned and run but the arm behind me was firm and unyielding.

"I married Jessie four years ago." The man's voice was quiet. "We are very happy." He hesitated, then, "You're Susan, aren't you?"

"I shouldn't have come back. It was stupid."

I wanted to escape but he was shaking his head.

"Susan," he said. "She told me all about you. Your photograph still stands in the middle of the mantelshelf. She has never forgotten."

"But he was shaking his head again. "Please," he said gently. "Please believe me. I know her. I love her. She's a wonderful person. And you could complete her happiness. She's always prayed you would come back, that one day she would see you again. We have no children of our own, you see."

I looked up into his face. His sincerity was unmistakable.

I hesitated just a moment more, then, with an enormous sense of relief, and with a stranger's arm, gentle but firm, urging me on, I stepped back into that garden, into her life. □

Dearly Beloved

He knew he was losing her so he turned for help to the only person in the world who really understood.

S NOW slowly spiralled round the amber street lights as Bob Foster drove home from the office. The cottage eaves in the village were fanged with icicles, the roofs snow covered like an old-world Christmas scene.

But Christmas had come and gone leaving Bob completely untouched by it.

His sister had invited him to spend the holiday with them, but bad weather had prevented him travelling.

He hadn't wanted to go anyway. Ever since Marcia had gone away, two-and-a-half years ago, he'd stopped celebrating Christmas in the old way.

When they had agreed to separate, Marcia had moved to London. He'd assumed, after the divorce, that she would have found the excitement and happiness she was searching for.

But, although she'd cleared all her personal property from the cottage they'd once shared, he still hadn't totally accepted that she'd gone for good. He wondered if he ever would.

"When routines become rituals, Bob, it's time to change your whole lifestyle."

Marcia had meant herself, of course. She never really wanted the family scene — had craved the bright lights. That was her nature.

They'd married in haste; now came his time for repentance, which looked like lasting for ever. He still lived in the cottage. He still went to the office where they'd first met.

DEARLY BELOVED

He remembered so well the time when he'd joined the firm. The London-based company had moved its head office to this rural area, creating many jobs for local people, people like himself.

Marcia had come with her job from London. Perhaps it had been inevitable — her return to the place where she belonged.

Bob sighed, peering through the fan-shaped area swept clean by the windscreen wipers, waiting for the headlights to show the turning to the cottage through the dancing snow.

He garaged the car, and was hardly across the threshold when the phone rang in the hall. He started unbuttoning his coat, lifting the receiver with his free hand. It was a man's voice, a stranger, from a call box.

"Mr Foster? Bob Foster?"

"Yes, who's speaking?"

"You won't know me, Mr Foster. My name's Lawson, Frank Lawson. You and I have something in common."

"I don't see how, I've never heard of you." There was something about this voice that put Bob on the defensive.

"I'm Marcia's husband."

Bob's fingers tightened round the receiver. "I don't understand!"

"It's perfectly simple. I married Marcia three months ago."

Bob took a deep breath, and tried his utmost to sound normal, as if this was an ordinary, everyday conversation.

"That's none of my business, is it? I haven't seen my wi — ex-wife, for —"

"Marcia is still very much your business. I must meet you, for your own sake."

"*My* sake? You're not making any sense!"

There was silence for a moment, then the stranger spoke again.

"Marcia's left me. And I've reason to believe she's with you."

Bob couldn't take it in. The strange voice came grimly over the wire.

"If you refuse to see me, then I'll be convinced she's with you."

"What?" Bob's astonishment gave way to anger. "Where are you, man?"

"In the phone box on the next corner. I can see your hall light from where I'm standing."

"So you could be ringing my doorbell within half a minute?"

"If that's an invitation, Mr Foster . . ."

The line went dead. Bob hung up, and mechanically went through the motions of preparing for a visitor, turning on the lights and fire in the living-room, clearing chairs and table.

The front doorbell rang. He stiffened, and moved reluctantly to the door.

The big man stamping his feet in the porch shelter wore a sheepskin coat with leather buttons, polished brogue shoes and leather gloves. His dark hair was powdered with snow; his eyes were watchful — apprehensive.

"Mr Foster?" He removed a glove, extending his right hand. The handshake was like a vice and left Bob's fingers tingling.

Bob closed the front door behind him, but remained in the hall. Frank Lawson seemed to fill the small space — a large, confident man. But he sounded strangely tentative.

"I didn't know how else to go about this. I don't really think my wife is here — I can see that in your eyes. But I had to be sure."

"Why?" Bob said coldly.

"I'm desperate. I have to find my wife. I don't want to drag a private detective into this . . . so I thought of you."

"But why me? I haven't seen Marcia since the day she left. As far as I know she's never been back this way."

The big man hovered uncertainly and Bob changed his mind. "Come in, for heaven's sake."

HE led the way into the lounge. Frank Lawson accepted a fireside chair, but sat stiffly on the edge of it.

"Marcia packed a case and disappeared just over a week ago. She left a note saying she had to get away. That was all."

"Have you contacted the police?"

"No! It's not like that . . . I know she's all right, but —"

"*How* do you know? If she was all right, she'd be —"

"Home with me?" Frank Lawson raised anguished eyes to Bob's.

"She should be, of course. And it's my fault. It's got to be, otherwise she wouldn't have gone off that way. But I don't know what I've done wrong!"

Bob was shaken. Those words were uncomfortable echoes from the past. Hadn't he said something like that, two-and-a-half years ago? And why, oh why, had Marcia remarried? She'd left *him* to get away from marriage — prison sentence, she'd called it.

Bob thrust old memories aside.

"I still don't understand why you've come to me. London's a long way."

"I don't care how far I have to travel if it means getting Marcia back." He paused, and added more quietly. "Marcia often talks of you." He shrugged. "I suppose comparisons were inevitable. And she has a very high regard for you. In fact, lately I've come to the conclusion that she thinks more of you than she does of —"

He broke off, and leaned forward suddenly, his whole body sagging.

"Would you like a drink?" Bob asked. "Coffee? Or something stronger?"

Gratefully, Frank Lawson answered, "Something stronger, please."

Bob sat opposite his visitor, warming his brandy glass in his hands, and waited. Frank Lawson didn't take long to pull himself together.

"I don't want to intrude in your life, Mr Foster. But it does seem to affect Marcia's relationship with me."

"I didn't even know she'd remarried. That's how much we've been out of touch."

DEARLY BELOVED

Frank Lawson sipped his drink as if it didn't agree with him.

"Perhaps she was too proud to tell you."

"Proud?"

"I knew she'd vowed never to remarry. So I was amazed — and delighted — when she said yes. I've known her for two years, but maybe she was still on the rebound . . ." He stared into his glass as if seeking inspiration. "In my job, Mr Foster, I have to sort out a lot of other people's problems, but this —"

"Does Marcia still work?"

"No. She stopped before we were married. I'm not short of money, she never wants for anything. We went to the Caribbean for our honeymoon . . . Marcia has her own car, a woman to help with the housework . . . We've a big place, you see."

"But . . . ?" Bob prompted.

"I thought I could provide her with everything. I know she's restless, but I couldn't help hoping —"

How well Bob understood that. There was silence for a moment.

"Well, where is she?" Bob said. "Where can she be? If she's run away *to* somebody, and it's not me, where is she?"

"I've contacted all her London friends. Believe me, I've neglected my business since she left. But no-one's heard from her."

Bob reached for a pipe and began filling it from his favourite pouch. Frank Lawson's plight intrigued him.

"How did you know where I lived?"

"Oh, that wasn't difficult. Marcia talked a lot about this village, this cottage." He glanced round the room, and back at Bob. "I drove down and made some discreet enquiries at the local pub."

"The Red Lion?"

Frank Lawson nodded. "I've booked a room. Don't fancy driving back to London in this weather."

Bob finished packing his pipe, and looked thoughtfully across at his visitor.

"Look, you caught me off-balance earlier. But you're right about one thing: Marcia is still my business. I'm sorry this has happened, but I'm sure Marcia married you for the right reasons."

"I appreciate the thought, but a wife doesn't go off after three months if she's happy."

"No," Bob said absently. A thought had just occurred to him. There was just one person who'd been close to Marcia when they'd split up . . .

But Frank Lawson was still lost in his own thoughts.

"I must confess, at first I was convinced Marcia had come back to you. But that was anger. Unreasonable." He set down his glass.

"I think I should leave now. I've taken advantage of your good nature. Marcia always says what an understanding sort of person you are.

"You'd have been quite justified in throwing me out. But I'm glad you didn't."

He stood up. "If I'd found Marcia here, I don't think I could have blamed her. We've had a lot of fights lately over the most trivial things. But, despite it all, I really thought she loved me, just as I love her."

He stood on one side of the hearth, large, bewildered, unhappy, and Bob faced him.

"I just wish I could help, but I've got an appointment this evening," Bob told him. "Perhaps I could see you later at The Red Lion? In two hours?"

Frank Lawson nodded.

"I'm going to have dinner there, and time on my hands. I'd be glad to buy you a drink later. You must think I'm crazy, coming all this way just for a glimpse of Marcia's past . . ."

He shook his head, picked up his gloves, thanked Bob for the drink, and on the way out, hesitated on the porch steps. The snow was gusting strongly, muffling sounds in the street. He glanced back to the warm, lighted room and added, "Just talking to you has helped, you know."

"You're no wiser than when you came, are you?" Bob raised his eyebrows.

"Well, I needed to see you. I think I've felt you were still a threat to me — and to Marcia."

He turned up his collar, slipped on his gloves. "Thanks for your time. I'll be in the bar of The Red Lion until closing time." He trudged off through the snow towards the blurred outline of a Mercedes parked halfway up the street.

Left alone in the hall, Bob stood by the phone.

Helen Jarvis.

Helen had never liked him. When he and Marcia had separated, she'd taken Marcia's side.

But Helen was the only person he knew who could link him with Marcia. And he had a funny feeling . . . instinct, perhaps?

He looked her up in the book, and dialled her number. He scarcely dared to breathe as he waited for a reply.

HELEN JARVIS didn't give her name or number, just a smoky: "Hello?"

"Helen?" Bob said uneasily.

"Speaking."

"Helen, this is Bob Foster. Marcia's ex-husband."

Silence.

"Hello? Helen?" Still a deafening silence.

"Yes, I heard you, Bob." Unfriendly now. "What did you want?"

"I'm sorry to disturb you, Helen." Bob licked his suddenly-dry lips. "It's about Marcia."

He could picture Helen's annoyed face, and her hesitation gave him the time he needed.

"Helen, it's your privilege to hang up on me, but I only want to know one thing."

"Which is?"

"Is Marcia there with you?"

He heard her sharp intake of breath, suddenly cut off, as if the mouthpiece had been covered. He closed his eyes, imagining Helen Jarvis consulting someone else in the room . . .

"Look, Bob!" She was back, blustering. "Why have you rung? I mean, you and I —"

"Let's top sparring, Helen. We never saw eye to eye. But I'd like to speak to Marcia — please — if she's with you?"

Another long pause — Bob was convinced he'd been right.

He heard a sigh at the other end, and then a voice said, "Bob?"

Not Helen Jarvis' voice now.

"Marcia?"

His pulse quickened, and he didn't conceal his pleasure.

"Marcia, you *are* there!"

"Yes. But how on earth did you know?"

She sounded guarded, but not unfriendly. He steadied himself for the lie.

"I heard at work. Someone happened to see you. So I rang up on the off-chance. How are you?"

"I'm OK. And you?"

"So-so. Look, I don't really want to impose on your time or Helen's, but —"

"Yes?"

"Any chance of seeing you?" He steeled himself for her reply. It was suddenly very important for him to see her. But she'd refuse, of course.

"I don't know, Bob. Right out of the blue . . . I'm intrigued, but —"

"I could call round for you. We could go for a drink, perhaps? Somewhere close by?"

Another long silence, mouthpiece covered again, then Marcia's tone altered.

"I could see you, but here would be more convenient."

"What about — ?"

"Helen? We can talk in the living-room. She says she'll make herself scarce . . . If you still want to come . . . ?"

"I'll come across now," he said.

Afterwards, driving across the snow-bound town, he was amazed at his own recklessness. Marcia had always been the reckless one; and how well he remembered her unpredictable outbursts. The prospect of seeing her again after all this time excited, unnerved him. But he couldn't turn back now. Briefly, he thought of Frank Lawson at The Red Lion.

H E'D expected Helen Jarvis to answer the door, but Marcia opened it.
She pulled it wide, despite the biting wind. In the ruddy glow of the hall lamp he found no words at first as he studied the woman who'd once been his wife.

Marcia was fashionably and expensively dressed. Her hair was in the same style, but she was fuller in the face.

"Bob."

Even before they shook hands, he was aware of her perfume. He'd half expected that to be the same, but it was unfamiliar; subtle, alien somehow.

"I'm glad to see you, Marcia."

He released her hand. Her fingers were as they'd always been, slim, dry and cool.

"Let me take your coat."

She hung up his coat, and the intimacy of the gesture pleased him. During the subsequent moments of awkward silence she kept staring up into his eyes. Then, wonderingly:

"I see it — but I don't believe it, Bob."

He shrugged, warming his hands on the hall radiator.

"Come in by the fire," she said, as if she'd surfaced from a trance. "It's horrible out there."

In the living-room, a log fire burned cheerfully. Marcia followed his gaze, and drew the heavy curtains, completing their privacy.

She turned, standing beside the window.

"You look well, Bob."

"And you. You look very fit — and very happy —"

She winced at that, moving to the fireside. She nudged one of the burning logs with the heel of her boot, offered him a seat and a drink, which he refused.

For several minutes they chatted uneasily, then he said:

"I hope I'm not putting Helen out, Marcia."

She shook her head. She looked elegant enough, but her hands were tightly clenched in her lap.

"When did you hear that I was back in town?"

"Less than an hour ago."

"Someone from the office, you said?"

"Not exactly, Marcia."

"Then who?"

She was balanced on the edge of her chair. Just as Frank Lawson had been sitting earlier.

"Your husband," he said. "Frank Lawson told me."

DEARLY BELOVED

She was instantly pale, suspicion hard in her eyes.

"Frank? He phoned you?"

"That's right. I didn't say so earlier, in case — well, I was afraid you wouldn't see me."

She unclenched her hands, holding both arms of the chair.

"But why lie to me, Bob?"

"Because —" He leaned forward. "I wanted to make sure your husband was genuine, that he was telling the truth."

"Truth?" She glanced at him. "What has Frank been telling you?"

"He thought you'd come back to me."

"But that's preposterous!"

"Your husband sounded pretty desperate to me, Marcia."

She flinched. Even in distress, she was lovely. He saw the shadows beneath her eyes, and was filled with sudden compunction.

"Look, Marcia, it's none of my business, but Frank Lawson seems mystified by your disappearance."

"It's not like that. I left a note. He knows I'd be all right." Her eyes narrowed.

"How did Frank get hold of you, anyway?"

"Well, he seemed to know about the village . . . some of the things that happened in the past?"

Twin spots of crimson touched her cheeks. She looked away.

"I've thought a lot about you, Marcia," he added. "I'm glad you remarried, found someone safe."

"Safe?" Her eyes flashed. "Bob. You and I lived a lifetime ago. I was young and green and thought I knew what I wanted . . ." She paused.

"When I went back to London, I did all the things I thought I wanted to do; acting in amateur dramatics, lots of parties with the old set, dancing every week — I painted the town red. But all the time I felt terribly lonely. Then I met Frank."

"Good!"

She shot him a reproving glance.

"It's natural for you to think that I was to blame for the split, Bob."

"I don't blame anyone. But I'm only human. I'm curious. Out of the blue, your second husband rings me up, practically accusing me of harbouring his wife?"

"I'm sorry, Bob. Frank shouldn't have —"

"My God, in his position I'd have done exactly the same thing! When you're demented with worry you have to clutch at any straw."

That had shaken her. Contrite, she said, "Thanks for making the effort, Bob —"

"Effort? Coming here? That's absolutely no trouble at all."

Their eyes met, and held.

"Bob — if only things could have been different between us, if only we'd met now, instead of years ago . . ."

Just then he could easily have crossed the hearth rug, taken her in his arms, held her close. But no.

"That's history," he said gruffly. "I thought you'd be here, that's all."

"I have nowhere else to go, Bob. Outside London . . ."

"That's what I hoped. I wanted to see you again, I'll admit that. When Frank Lawson first rang I was angry. Then I realised that I needed to see you again, if only —"

"Go on."

"If only to convince myself you were happy."

"Bob, I've just packed a bag and run out on my husband. D'you call that being happy?"

"I call that being reckless. But then, you always were unpredictable."

She sank deeper into her chair, suddenly very frail and vulnerable.

"It's eerie, Bob. When the phone rang earlier, I wasn't at all surprised that it was you."

"Oh?"

A sad smile tugged at her mouth.

"In a way, I was glad, too, when you suggested meeting me. I've wondered a lot about you; worried, as well.

"Helen occasionally wrote, but all she said was that you were working in the same place, and you'd never remarried."

She leaned back in her chair.

"Helen thinks I'm better off without any contact with the past. But she was understanding enough to agree to your coming here tonight. Ever since I arrived I've toyed with the idea of ringing you."

"I'd have hated it if you hadn't."

She nodded, then lapsed into a sullen, unhappy silence.

"What will you do now?"

She pulled a face.

"Helen's offered to let me stay here, but —"

"She has her own life to lead?"

MARCIA stared into the flames again. Since he'd first set eyes on her in the hall, minutes ago, she seemed to have aged dramatically. Her eyes were sombre, her head bent in misery.

"Marcia, what is it? Can you tell me?"

She raised her head painfully slowly, met his eyes, and her own filled with tears.

"Oh, Bob, I've made such a mess of things . . . first my marriage to you, and now —"

"It takes two to quarrel. And two to become incompatible."

"I know." Tears rolled unchecked down her cheeks. "But with

DEARLY BELOVED

Frank, I've got myself into such a state. He's given me everything I ever wanted or needed — but we've rowed so much lately. And now —"

Bob took out his handkerchief and handed it to her. She dried her cheeks, but her eyes still brimmed with tears.

"I'm a coward, Bob, you know that? An arrant coward. I was always so outward looking, so blatant, so sure of myself. And now, I can't relate to Frank, at the very time when I should most of all be able to —"

She hesitated, then blurted out, "I'm pregnant, Bob."

A log settled in the grate, raising sparks. Bob placed a hand firmly on her shoulder, and said:

"That's fantastic! And I'm not surprised."

She raised a tear-stained face to his.

"You're not?"

"Well, I should have guessed, Marcia. You have that look about you." He ignored her sceptical expression.

"You look — well, more mellow!" He managed a grin.

Her shoulder trembled beneath his fingers and reluctantly he removed his hand.

"So that's what you couldn't tell your husband?"

"Oh, Bob, you make it sound so ordinary! But we've only just got married. Frank didn't bargain for kids, not yet. He likes me looking beautiful, the perfect hostess — he entertains so many clients at home, you see.

"And I'm not ready for children. I haven't even settled properly with Frank. I slid into this marriage . . . I need more time. Oh, the problems we've had recently!"

"Look, love," Bob interrupted. "You know I've always been the over-cautious type. But I'd bet my pension that if Frank Lawson knew he was going to become a father he'd be —"

He stopped. Marcia wasn't listening. The handkerchief was a soggy muddle in her lap.

"Does Helen know?"

She nodded, without enthusiasm.

"I had to tell someone."

"Then it's high time your husband knew."

She glared at him, stung by the sharpness of his tone.

"I'm sorry, Marcia. It may not be any of my business, but I'd have thought the father had a right to know."

She heaved a deep wretched sigh.

"However did I get myself into such a state, Bob? The prospect of telling Frank terrifies me."

"Tell him now. I know that if it had been me —" He broke off, annoyed. Had he given himself away?

"I'm scared, Bob. After going off like that . . . leaving Frank so soon after the wedding. But I had to find some time to think — get my feelings straight."

She looked up, and went on, "It's not something you talk about over the telephone . . ." Her tone was serious.

"Then why not tell him in person? Right now?"

She looked mystified.

"He's here, Marcia. Go and wash your face, and I'll take you to him."

"Will you please explain, Bob?" she implored, sitting beside him in the car as he steered cautiously back through the driving snow.

IT'S simple. Frank Lawson's in the bar of The Red Lion Inn. And I'm delivering you to him safe and sound."

"Bob? I don't —"

"I've already met him."

"But you said he phoned you from London!"

"He phoned me, but not from London. Did I say he phoned from London? And if I was him I'd tan your hide."

"Bob!" She was half laughing. "It's no good, I can't understand. I'm bewildered."

"So is your husband. For starters, you might look like you're glad to see him. He can fill in the rest of the explanations!"

He gave her a hard sideways glance. The fur coat was sumptuous, its collar caressing her cheeks, her hair gleamed, her big haunting eyes . . .

"Marcia, you look marvellous!" he said gruffly.

He pulled into The Red Lion car park and helped her out. A few flakes of snow settled on her eyelashes, melting instantly into tears. He took her inside the pub that had been their local, and stopped by the glass door leading into the lounge.

At the same moment, they both saw Frank Lawson standing at the tinselled bar, one foot on the rail, staring gloomily in front of him.

Marcia caught her breath.

"Go on," Bob whispered. "Go to him. He's come a long way for you. You could at least meet him halfway across that carpet."

He lingered, watching, as she went into the bar, took a few tentative steps. Frank Lawson noticed her. His face filled with astonishment, relief, joy. His shoulders straightened, and he came towards her . . .

Bob turned away and went out to his car. He'd lost Marcia once before; in a way, he'd lost her again tonight. They'd never had a family . . . they'd missed out on so many things.

He watched the snow spiralling round the amber street lamps, the eaves fanged with icicles, the roofs snow-covered like an old-world Christmas scene.

Christmas may be over, he thought, but he'd to go to his sister's, whatever the weather. And Marcia's voice nudged him from somewhere far away:

When routines become rituals, Bob, it's time to change your whole lifestyle!

She was right, of course. He sighed, got into his car, and drove home. □

Complete Story By **SARAH PARKES**

A PLACE IN THEIR HEARTS

Why didn't they stop treating her like a child and tell her the truth?

MARGARET sat in the small back sitting-room with the door half open, listening to the baby screaming upstairs. He'd been like this, on and off, for the last couple of days. She'd thought he was teething, and as luck would have it, his favourite cuddly toy, Bert the bunny, was

H

missing. It was always the one he found comfort from — it worked magic!

Outside in the garden, Margaret could hear the lawn-mower. George was busy in his beloved garden. She knew the lawn was near perfect and wondered if he should be exerting himself, but at least the lawn was flat, and the mower a motor-driven one.

There was silence upstairs now and she realised Robbie was asleep. Now she could hear the two girls laughing in the front room — Julie and her friend Kate. It was a silly giggling sound, but she was just pleased to hear them happy.

Suddenly the lounge door banged open, followed by the crash of the girls careering out into the hall. the front door was opened and shut again as Kate ran off home.

"Julie," Margaret called out.

But already her daughter was halfway up the stairs.

She called again. "Julie!"

The girl came down and appeared in the doorway. She'd been in a strange mood lately, distant and rather sullen. Margaret put it down to growing up, but was becoming tired of her daughter's moods on top of Robbie's upset.

Julie stood tapping her foot impatiently. "What did you want me for, Mum?" she asked hurriedly. "I want to go and change."

"Oh!" Margaret couldn't hide her disappointment at her daughter's off-handedness. "I was thinking of having a coffee, and wondered if you'd like one, too."

"No, thanks. Kate and I had a drink earlier. Where's Dad? He might want one." She glanced out of the window, catching sight of her father bending over the mower. "He's forever cutting the grass. 'Bye, Mum, I must go. I'm meeting Kate at three o'clock."

She doesn't mean to be short, Margaret assured herself.

"I thought perhaps you'd be able to give me a hand with some ironing, but instead we could walk up to Kate's house together, when Robbie wakes up. I've some shopping to do."

Julie didn't asnwer immediately, and Margaret began to feel the smile on her face was stretching and rather foolish. "Well?"

"Couldn't Dad go shopping with you? He's nothing else to do."

"Julie!"

But Julie had gone, and minutes later Margaret heard the outside door. When George came in, five minutes later, she rose to make a coffee.

"I'm getting on slowly," she said, grinning wryly. "The room looks a mess, but I'm just about to start the ironing."

"Couldn't Julie have done something for once?" he asked. "You should insist. And where is she? I wondered if she'd be going out. I have a prescription to take down to the chemist." He sat down.

"Are you all right? You shouldn't be out so long in the hot sun." Margaret looked at him anxiously.

"Don't fuss."

"Robbie will be awake very soon. He's being a bit weepy at the moment. He's lost his precious bunny and it's the first thing he looks for when he wakes. I remember he had it on Tuesday when Julie took him to the park. I wondered if he had thrown it out of his pushchair."

"Have you asked Julie?"

"Oh, no," Margaret said quickly. "I don't want her to think it's her fault that it's lost."

They sat in silence for a moment. Margaret's mind had been in a turmoil since Julie had rushed out, and she could no longer hold back.

"George, what's gone wrong in this house lately? Robbie has started this screaming, Julie is not her usual self, and all on top of you having been ill! What's to be done?"

"Julie is lazy," her father said.

"I thought it would be such fun for her when I was expecting Robbie. I knew there'd be difficulties with the age gap, but do you remember how excited she was? And when Robbie was born, she chose the name. We made up our minds then, that she should never feel pushed aside by Robbie.

I T was such fun at first sharing in the feeding and taking him out and bathing him. She loved to help. I'd decided that I'd never ask her help, but look at her now! She's changed so much. Could it just be a phase she's going through?"

"Are you sure that it's only Julie that has changed?" George asked. "You're so tired out. Having a toddler at this stage in our lives hasn't been too easy. And you had me to nurse as well. Perhaps you've lost a bit of patience for the moment."

"I'm worrying about your job as well. George, suppose you're not able to take your job on again? You know, Julie doesn't know all this. We didn't want to worry her. She just thinks that you're having an extra holiday after a virus."

"Perhaps we should have told her the truth, Margaret. After all, she's no longer a child."

"I want her to be happy," she said firmly. "Not worried by things that needn't concern her."

He got up. "I'll walk to the chemist myself."

She had just begun to sort and fold the clothes ready for ironing, when she heard Robbie crying.

She hurried upstairs, and before he had time to miss his toy, she cuddled him to her and hurried downstairs. She settled him in his chair with his favourite drink and then turned to get on with her ironing. She managed to get quite a lot done before Robbie became restless.

"Walk," he gurgled. "P'am," he said, pointing out to his pushchair in the corner.

It was a relief to get out into the fresh air, and she lingered for a while in the park, keeping a lookout for a soft bunny toy. But there was no sign of it. She turned again for home, and was soon preparing Robbie's tea.

A PLACE IN THEIR HEARTS

The evening sun was streaming into the kitchen. She felt more cheerful now. She put out some chocolate biscuits for Julie, and was about to pour herself a cup of tea when she heard the door.

"Julie!"

Julie burst into the kitchen. "Where's Dad?"

"I don't know. He went out to the chemist's. I expect he's . . ."

"You don't know!" Julie accused. Her voice was trembling. Margaret was taken aback

at her rage. Then Julie burst out, "You never told me!"

"Told you what?" Margaret asked, bewildered.

"I didn't know that Dad was still ill, that he might have to retire. I had tea at Kate's. Her father came in and he talks to me as if I'm grown up. He mentioned how worried we must all be. How was I to know! You never told me."

"We didn't want you to worry."

"Do you think I'm still a child? Mum, I'm fourteen."

Margaret put out her hands towards her daughter but Julie stepped back.

"You don't tell me anything, anything. I can't help — I'm nothing, nothing."

She ran back into the hall. Her mother heard her voice.

"Dad! I didn't hear you come in. Are you all right? Mum's made a pot of tea. You go in and have some. I'm going ouside for a bit."

"What's the matter with her?" George asked as he came into the room. "Julie looked so angry just now, yet changed whenever she saw me. I don't know what she's up to, but she's gone outside."

He turned to play with Robbie, who was toying with a crust. The youngster laughed as George pretended to take it from him and eat it.

"She's just heard about you, from Kate's father. He told her how ill you've been and it's upset her. She blames me. You were right, George. We should have told her."

George was about to voice his agreement when a noise from the garden made him rush over to the window.

"Good Lord!" he exclaimed. "It's Julie, finishing the grass. Look, Margaret. Would you believe it?"

They stood together watching her marching behind the lawn-mower with a great deal of determination. Margaret didn't know whether she was nearer to tears or laughter. She picked up Robbie and hugged him as she took him over to the window. He waved jammy fingers at Julie, who looked up and gave a glimmer of a smile.

Half an hour later, as Margaret was kneeling beside Robbie's bath, she heard Julie come in. She heard George's voice as the pair of them talked in the hall downstairs. Julie's voice came floating up the stairs to her as Robbie splashed happily.

"Oh, all right then, Dad. I'll lay the table. It's just that Mum never really asks me for any help."

Margaret lifted the baby from the bath and powdered him. He was warm, pink and sweet. She counted his fingers and played with his toes, saying silly things to him as she pinned his nappy and fastened him into his sleepsuit.

She carried him to his cot and laid him down. No sooner had she done this when he sat up and waved his arms.

"Lie down," she told him. "Come on now! It's sleep you're needing."

Turning, she saw Julie in the doorway. "Isn't he an angel?"

But Julie wasn't smiling. "I laid the table like Dad said. But I don't know what you've got for a sweet."

Margaret could sense it hadn't been easy for her daughter to come to her. "Well now," she began, "shall we have . . ."

But Robbie had suddenly scrambled to his feet and was rattling the bars of his cot. He was pointing with one hand, vaguely, but definitely something was distracting him.

MARGARET was still trying to figure out what was wrong, when Julie moved across the room.

"He keeps doing this. Whenever he wakes or when I've just laid him down, he's so upset. I can only think it's because he's lost that bunny. You know, Bertie, we called it."

"But Bert-Bunny is up there, Mum, where he's pointing, on top of the wardrobe. I saw it there yesterday." Julie climbed on the stool to reach the woolly toy.

"I never thought of looking up there. I was so sure you'd lost it when you took him to the park the other day."

"If only you had asked me! I could have told you yesterday. I thought he'd chucked it there and I climbed up to get it down. But then I thought perhaps you'd put it there deliberately because you didn't like the way he chews its ears all the time."

Suddenly the room was quiet as Robbie settled down under the coverlet, Bunny beside his little pink face, the tip of one cloth ear stuffed into his mouth.

"Look, Mum! Isn't he lovely?"

They stood together for a moment.

"You should have told me, Mum," Julie whispered.

"I'll tell you something now — you choose the sweet!"

Julie smiled. "We'll have ice-cream from the freezer." Julie tiptoed from the room and rushed off downstairs.

"Come on, Dad. I'm dishing up the vegetables," Margaret heard her call.

As Robbie closed his eyes, she turned to follow Julie downstairs. ☐

When the sun shines up at Croft Douglas it's hay-making time, with the swish of the scythe and the sweet smell of summer in the air.

By Gideon Scott May

WHEN the summer morning is mirrored in minute detail on the surface of the loch and there are fragile fragments of mist drifting daintily here and there, like the cast-away wrappings from a gift, it's a beautiful sunny hay day. And, as the glinting dewdrops are drying, fanned by the breath of a light morning breeze, we carefully sharpen our scythes, with old Finlay's words ringing in my ears.

"Laddie, you'll never scythe until you can sharpen." He always calls me laddie, and it keeps me years younger than I am.

So the stone slides caressingly up one side of the blade and down the other, as we carefully sharpen the scythe to cut the hay the old-fashioned way.

There's a host of wild-life in our little hay field. They are the fortunate few who won't be terrorised by the rough, raucous chatter of a reaper.

The soft whisper of the scythe says slowly, and regretfully, that it's time for all furred and feathered folk to find shelter somewhere else.

There's a pair of partridges who have nested here. They're moving about just in front of the blade, so I pause to give them a little time to think things out and make their next move.

The cock bird steps out first. You can always tell him by the bold chestnut coloured horseshoe stamped on his breast and, with a quick right and left look, decides that the time has come to conduct his family to pastures new.

He gives a soft, reassuring "churr" to his mate and out comes the hen surrounded by what looks like a host of multi-coloured bumble bees. She wears a more modest dress, cleverly designed to camouflage and deceive predators, but she still manages to look pretty with her feathers preened to perfection.

Partridges are among the best parents in the bird world. The cock bird takes his turn to look after the large family whilst his mate has a well-earned "wander" and forgets, for a while, the demands of domesticity and the calling and caring for children.

She sifts every grain of sandy soil through her feathers and sighs at the thought that she mustn't overdo things and keep her model husband waiting too long.

For today is serious stuff, the family has to move and the parents, between them, carefully shepherd their children to the nearby "steep" field. It has not been cut this year and there is plenty of grass and

Making

clover to give their babies cover from high-flying hawks.

Young rabbits race out at regular intervals. They are almost half grown and out on their own. Mother is expecting another batch of babies!

But the young rabbits don't mind, they're experiencing the exciting feeling of independence and treat this sudden moving of house as fun.

There's a dainty roe deer fawn suddenly awakened from a short sleep, unsure where it is and what is happening. But Mother is watching and waiting by the woodside.

With a series of short, sharp barks she guides the frightened fawn to the safety of her side.

I PAUSE again for a moment to survey something just in front of the scythe's next sweep. It's a pair of leverets lying side by side, like little furry slippers their velvet ears lined with pink that seem to be buttoned to the small, silky, brown backs.

The only movement is fractional, just a nervous twitch of a tiny nose.

So the scythe carefully cuts a sheltering circle around them. The mother hare won't be far away and, on her return, will find her babies still safely tucked in the cosy cradle she so carefully made for them.

Visitors from the South are more than a little amazed by the long light of day we have here in the North, and providing the weather is kind, haymaking can be carried on throughout the momentary shadow that is sent at this time of year to represent night and dulls the glint on the hay forks for just a second before the dawn takes over and shakes the shoulder of the sun who, literally, hasn't had a wink of sleep and reluctantly rises again to supply yet another sizzling hot hay day.

Although the grasses are still green, like the preparation of a good meal, they must not be exposed to intense heat for the risk of burning. So, as soon as it's dry, we toss the green grass on to tripods of strong birch branches and build a series of conical coles which will preserve the goodness of the grasses, while the birch branches invite any passing breezes to go in and cool the heart of the cole and prevent any internal heating of the hay's juices.

Sometimes, when our hay crop is not a heavy one, we have to buy baled hay, made the commercial way. You only have to poke your nose into the baled hay shed, then into the barn of the carefully collected grasses, to know the difference.

Our hay has a sweet, seductive smell, so fresh and wholesome. No wonder the Highland cattle race to be at the head of the queue! □

GIDEON'S WAY

Hay

119

Complete Story By
DOROTHY L. GARRARD

Little Gentle Deception

**She knew too much about life not to recognise a
white lie when she heard one — or to go
along with it . . .**

B ETTY FILBERT awoke on Friday morning to the sound of
lashing rain on her bedroom window. She lay contemplating
the inevitable damp patch on the ceiling with resignation.

These days you simply couldn't find a handyman to come and
attend to the little jobs an elderly lady couldn't cope with, even if
you had the money.

In any case that cracked roof-tile was irreplaceable, a neighbour
from the other end of the terrace had told her so. These old houses
had been tiled with a job lot by the original small builder, and the
tiles were now obsolete.

Perhaps when Terry called today he'd be kind enough to take a
look in the loft and see if he could do anything. Though she didn't
really want to trouble him on the day he was driving halfway across
the country to bring his new fiancée, Jean, to tea.

Dear Terry, the only one, out of the procession of children who'd

121

passed through her house, who still cared and came to visit her.

Some still sent her Christmas cards, some had lost touch — but she was grateful for the memories they'd left her, and doubly grateful for Terry's continuing thoughtfulness.

Miss Filbert had dearly wanted to foster a child, but the lack of a husband disqualified her for anything long term. Honorary aunt, that's what she'd been, both to neighbours' and friends' children, and to those from a local children's home.

But for a long time now she'd been unable to find the energy to cope with their high spirits, to climb the local hills for picnics or play bears on the hearthrug.

Sometimes she wondered if she was too out of touch with the modern world to get along with them like she used to. Apparently the simple things didn't satisfy children any more.

She didn't lie in bed for long, because there were last-minute things to do before Terry and Jean arrived, such as unearth her best cutlery, and rinse the bone-china tea service ready for use.

The damp didn't help her creaky bones. She patiently struggled with her buttons, then went downstairs.

She put her porridge on the stove before discovering the milkman hadn't yet been — she'd used all her surplus last night, making the blancmange to top the trifle. She was awkwardly investigating the lower cupboard for a tin of milk substitute, when the telephone rang.

Terry's voice always took her by surprise, it was so deep and manly. It seemed only yesterday he'd worn his first pair of long trousers.

"Aunt Betty? I'm terribly sorry, but I think I'm going down with flu. I'm afraid I'll have to postpone the visit."

"Oh, what a shame . . . I'm so sorry you don't feel well," Miss Filbert said sympathetically, trying to hide her disappointment.

"Are you all right, Aunt Betty?"

"I'm fine, dear, fine."

"Good . . . I'm truly sorry about today, and so's Jean, she was looking forward to meeting you. I'll ring you when I feel better — OK?"

"Yes, dear, of course. Take care. Love to Jean."

THE smell of burning porridge floated from the kitchen. It was obviously going to be one of those days. She salvaged the remains, ate it with no milk and extra sugar, and scoured the pan painstakingly.

All week she'd been cleaning and polishing, because she wanted Terry and Jean to see the place at its best, and not notice the shabbiness. In the second-hand fridge — which that nice Mr Forest at the Sixty Club had obtained for her — reposed an exotic trifle, only waiting for a sprinkle of hundreds and thousands at the last minute so the colours wouldn't spread. And in the cake tin, a rich, sticky gingerbread confection made especially for Terry.

She would have shopped this morning for some fresh salad vegetables, and opened the tin of red salmon she'd been hoarding for ages for a special occasion like this.

But now, suddenly, there seemed nothing more to do. Her little house was quiet. Too quiet.

She switched on the radio and looked around for her knitting, then remembered she'd finished Terry's birthday pullover and hadn't decided what to knit next. Anyway, who wanted to start knitting at this time of morning?

The radio batteries were failing. A melancholy love song filtered through the hiss and crackle — "And now . . . that rainy day is here . . ."

"You'd better believe it!" Miss Filbert observed aloud. The slangy expression was an indication of her upset feelings.

Switching off the radio, she decided the situation called for an extra cup of tea.

As she reached for the tea caddy, she paused. On her kitchen dresser stood a jam-jar covered with sticky-backed plastic, which she'd bought from the Sunday school stall at the Christmas Fête.

It was a money-box, the child behind the counter had explained, pointing out the slot in the lid.

Miss Filbert had smiled. "I'll save my pennies in it for a rainy day!"

She picked up the jar thoughtfully. She had put her five pences — tiddlers, she called them — into the jar. If she found a money-saving coupon for groceries, she would slip the equivalent pence into the slot. And sometimes if she walked home from the Sixty Club, aided of course, by her faithful walking stick, she would put in the bus fare saved. The jar had stood there for some time, unopened.

Not wanting to spoil a child's handiwork, she found a flexible knife and emptied the jar on to the kitchen table.

Hardly a fortune! She could buy new radio batteries. Or wool. But she'd do that come pension day, anyway.

She played with the whimsical idea of rainy-day savings. What could one do with them — except go out in the rain to spend them!

She went to the window and contemplated the small back yard. The rain had abated slightly, the sky was getting lighter, and she had a raincoat, umbrella and wellington boots.

She'd be better outside than in, brooding on her disappointment.

"Come along, Betty!" she told herself firmly. "Get mobile, as Terry used to say!"

As an afterthought she changed some of the silver for pounds from her milk money before putting on her outdoor things.

Where should she go? There was nothing to do in the village on a wet Friday afternoon, so she'd catch the first bus which came along. Let Fate choose!

Standing well back from the kerb, waiting for the bus to come along, Miss Filbert noticed a large, black car heading towards town.

Wasn't that Mr Forest's car? What a pity he hadn't noticed her, she'd have enjoyed a nice chat on the way to town.

A LITTLE GENTLE DECEPTION

She'd met Mr Forest some time ago at the Sixty Club, but he was an infrequent attender, so she'd never got to know him really well.

Well, after all, this *was* a rainy day excursion, and there was sure to be a bus along soon.

The first bus was going all the way to Bellchester — about an hour's ride.

Slowly, she sat down, arranging her mac so the drips didn't fall into her wellingtons, and peered through the blurred windows at the dripping countryside, willing the rain to cease before she reached the terminus.

IN Bellchester, the weather had compromised by diminishing to a slight drizzle.

She walked briskly along the main street, aiming for the covered market where she spent some time browsing among the stalls.

She treated herself to a card of fancy buttons for use on her next cardigan, instead of resorting to her used-button box, and went out of the far exit.

She noticed a small boy idling near a doorway, over which a cloth banner hung dejectedly.

Maritime Exhibition, it read. *Admission £1. Children half price. Refreshments available.*

The child was marching up and down, peering at the pavement. Impulsively she asked, "What are you looking for?"

"A fifty-pence piece," he said briefly.

He had bright dark eyes and a cheeky turned-up nose, reminding her vaguely of Terry.

She helped him look along the puddled pavement, without success.

"It could have rolled down the drain," she said at last. "Did you want to see the exhibition?"

He nodded mutely, staring at the gushing river in the gutter.

"Come along then," she said briskly. It was so nice to be able to give a child a treat again. "I'll take you in."

He followed her very closely.

The man at the entrance desk peered round her, trying to take a look at the child behind her.

"Pardon my asking, madam, but do you know this young man?" he asked.

"Not exactly — we've only just met," she said, surprised. "He dropped his money outside, so . . ."

The child was sidling away, but, sensing a mystery, she took hold of his sleeve.

"Wait a minute! What's all this about?" She asked curtly.

The official shook his head. "Every day this week he's been in here! Paid for himself a couple of times, then I suppose the money ran out. He waits around for someone to fall for his hard-luck story!

"I can't keep on letting him come in with strangers, not when he knows I know what he's doing . . . encouraging him in deceitfulness, like. Can't just let him in either — I know it's only fifty pence, but my job's to collect admission. Do it for one, and . . ."

She looked severely at the child, who was surveying his shoes intently.

"It's wrong to tell lies," she reproved him gently.

"But I didn't!" he said, and with such certainty that she mentally ran over the conversation and realised that he hadn't lied.

"But you led me to think you'd lost your money, and that's the same thing. This gentleman says you've already seen the exhibition."

"But I wanted to see it again."

"Can't you save your pocket money?"

"I used it all, coming in. Mum won't advance me any, and I've got to go out with her tomorrow. And that's the last day, they'll take it all away, the boats and photographs and charts . . ."

The wistfulness in his eyes as he looked past her was no lie.

She followed his gaze through the open door of the first exhibition room, and caught a glimpse of model boats and ships in bottles.

"Do you know much about boats?"

"Yes! I'm going to be a sailor!"

"Well, I don't know a thing, and those labels they stick on showcases are always too tiny for my poor eyes to read. I'll pay for you, if you'll tell me all about it. Is that a bargain?"

He nodded eagerly.

"What's your name?" she asked, paying for the tickets.

"Tony."

"Well, Tony, I'm in your hands."

He led her eagerly inside.

"This room shows you the boats they made before there were shipyards and things. They used to hollow out logs at first, then they built frames and put skins round them. They called that sort a coracle," he told her importantly.

She was more intrigued by Tony's enjoyment than with the exhibition itself, but mindful of the idea that he should feel he was earning his admission, she got him to read out some of the small typed labels. Where a word defeated him, he spelled it for her and she told him what it meant.

They saw half-decked vessels such as Columbus used, the flagship of the Armada, a paddle-wheeled steamboat, fully-rigged clippers and screw-propelled liners.

After that, he conducted her through the chart room, full of maps and descriptions of navigation methods, ancient and modern. A long connecting gallery full of photographs led to a further room illustrating sea warfare, with exhibits borrowed from museums.

A LITTLE GENTLE DECEPTION

MISS FILBERT emerged at the end trying to disguise from this fresh young enthusiast the fact that her head was spinning.

"We don't have to go yet, do we?" he asked anxiously. "Couldn't we go back to the beginning?"

She looked at her wristwatch.

"It's long past lunch-time!" she cried guiltily. "Your mother will be wondering where you are! She'll be angry with you."

He shook his head. "My mum is at work all day. I brought some sandwiches but I got hungry before you came."

"Well, I expect you could eat something else now. I know I'm hungry. Where is the refreshment place?"

He conducted her to it. She had intended buying herself a cheese sandwich, but somehow found herself in possession of a hot dog, with a dubious thick red sauce squelching from the sides of it.

"Super!" Tony said.

He washed his down with cola, but she resisted his recommendations this time, and bought herself a strong cup of tea.

Politely, he tried not to fidget as she sipped it.

Presently she said, "You've kept your side of the bargain. Tony. I've really enjoyed the exhibition, but my legs are too tired to walk any more. I'll have to be going home soon."

Looking at him across the table, the years seemed to slip away, and she found herself surprised and gratified, knowing her easy ways with small boys hadn't deserted her.

She gave him a gentle push on the arm, the affectionate token she used to give Terry when he was too big to want kisses any more.

"Off you go and enjoy yourself."

He grinned, pushed back his chair with an excruciating scrape and hurried away.

Then he came running back. "Thanks. For the hot dog, and that." He gave her an embarrassed thump on the arm and darted away.

When her legs were rested, she reached for her walking stick and went outside. The rain had stopped, and there was a glimpse of blue sky above the market-place. She cut through to the bus stop, and noticed that many of the stall-holders seemed to have given up and gone home.

As she stood on the kerb by the bus shelter, a black car drew up alongside.

"Miss Filbert? Would you like a lift home?"

She recognised the grey hair and silvery moustache of Mr Forest, and climbed in beside him gratefully. Her legs had stiffened after the long rest.

"I saw you pass through the market before lunch," he told her, "but I couldn't attract your attention."

"You were shopping?"

"I was helping my son on his electrical goods stall. He has a small business in the next town and he's trying to expand it — believes in going where the trade is — but he didn't have much luck today."

"I expect the weather put people off. Did he pack up early?"

"That's right. Mind you, I don't often stay past mid-afternoon anyway, except in the summer now and then. The market's a draughty place for elderly bones!"

"I know," she agreed feelingly. "I'll probably pay for this excursion with a few extra twinges."

"Do you often come to Bellchester? I'd have thought it was rather out of your way."

"It is . . ." She found herself telling him about her disappointment over Terry, though not about the rainy-day savings.

"I expect it sounds rather silly of me to come out in such weather when I didn't need to," she finished apologetically. "But you have a family, I don't suppose you're alone very much. Your daughter lives with you, doesn't she?"

"Not now. Jenny's a career girl, determined to get to the top of her profession. She had the offer of a job in America and decided it was the next step up the ladder, so she flew to the States last month."

"So you're alone in the house, too."

"That's right — just like you." He gave her a comradely grin. "I'll be coming to the Sixty Club more often now, I expect. In any case, it's good to have companions of your own age."

She debated silently for a few moments, then asked, "Do you happen to like trifle, Mr Forest? With pink blancmange, flaked almonds, and a touch of chocolate?"

"Can't say I've tasted one exactly to that recipe, but by the sound of it, I've missed something rather special!"

"The fact is, I made it for Terry and Jean. It'll take me days to get through it by myself, and it won't be the same . . ."

"Are you inviting me to tea, Miss Filbert?"

"If you've time to stay, Mr Forest."

By the time tea was over, they were on Christian-name terms. After all, you couldn't demolish a raspberry trifle between you and still stay formal.

And before he left, Ted Forest climbed into the loft to take a look at the tile problem.

"Well, I can't replace the tile, Betty, but I'll bring some stuff along to seal up the gap. And this plastic bucket under it until I come should save another wet ceiling.

"Meanwhile — see you at the Sixty Club on Monday?"

"I never miss it," she assured him.

When he'd gone, she emptied her purse on to the table. A fifty pence piece remained from the Rainy-Day Fund.

Perhaps one day she'd tell Ted this part of it too. How she'd lived and learned, taken a step back into a happy past with a small boy, and made a new friend.

Smiling, she went to drop the coins back into the jar, a starter for the next rainy day. But she was quite sure there'd never be another one quite like this. □

Once Upon A Summer

**A bright future beckoned,
but first she had to take one last look at a very
important part of her past.**

IT was too early in the season for many visitors, and I was grateful for that as I left the mainland and drove across the causeway to the Holy Island of Lindisfarne.

I had thought of walking over, but remembering my last visit I knew I couldn't face it.

My heart thumped loudly as I passed the place of refuge by the central bridge. Wasn't this where it had begun all those years ago?

"I must be mad to return here. Whatever made me do it?" I muttered to myself in a frenzy as I drove into the car park, in two minds whether or not to turn back.

I was glad of the warmth of my jacket and of my scarf. The cold wind was relentless

The island isn't very big. I was pleased there were no coaches today; too many trippers would spoil the atmosphere, though I don't remember thinking that on my previous visit.

High tide had been at eight this morning, so I'd had to wait until after eleven to cross when the causeway was clear. It would be quite safe up to two hours before second high tide, so I would need to leave before six this evening; though I didn't anticipate staying that long.

I made my way towards the ruins of Lindisfarne Priory. There it stood after all these centuries, framed majestically against the blue sky, just as I remembered it.

I felt the surge of that age-old wish to turn back the clock, but it was soon lost in the jumble of my thoughts, like grains of sand in the wind.

I turned away from the ruins, and went instead to the centuries-old church. Today I was in search of a little peace and shelter from the wind.

There were perhaps half a dozen tourists wandering round as I entered. The air was filled with the fresh fragrance of flowers. There were vases of sweet peas and roses all round, on every available ledge.

I sat near the back and took out a photograph of my son. He was only three, but the eyes that smiled back were those of his father.

As I sat on the hard wooden bench, I let my mind wander back to four years ago . . .

TWO friends had asked me to join them in their two-week holiday in a caravan at Beadnell Bay. They warned me not to expect much, as it was a very small place and even in the middle of the season could be very quiet. And they would be occupied, most of the time, on a local archaeological dig.

At the beginning of the first week we'd all joined a coach trip to Holy Island. They were discussing beginning their dig the next day, when I first noticed the dark, handsome boy sitting up beside the driver. Several times I felt him watching me and then he made a point of helping me from the coach.

"Hi. My name's Graham. I'm here on holiday staying with my uncle. I've been to the island many times before. How about letting me show you round?"

How could I refuse that disarming smile and the laughter in those intense blue eyes?

There had been a two-way magic right from that first moment. It wasn't long before we broke away from the party and the guide, as did some of the others.

"Let's go and visit the castle, Rachel. I know you'll like it. It was built in the sixteenth century, but it's now been converted into a private house."

He led me away between the hundreds of lobster pots and old boathouses, towards Lindisfarne Castle.

We began to weave dreams round the fairy-tale castle as we approached it. It had such a romantic image, rising as it did from the stony beach and sand dunes. Graham clasped my hand as we climbed the winding path up to its entrance.

As we went from room to room, he whispered in my ear, making me laugh. He even pretended it was our home, acting as Lord of the Manor, causing other tourists to stare, some smiling knowingly, others showing their distaste at our frivolity.

The day passed all too quickly. We had to hurry back to the coach before the rising tide covered the causeway, and cut us off from the mainland.

That had only been the beginning of what turned out to be a wonderful holiday. I saw Graham every day after that and never did get to join the girls on their "dig", seeing them briefly each night and morning only.

There was little of that coastline we didn't explore, seeking out the isolated beaches, far from the other tourists.

On warm days we ran barefoot, chasing the receding tide or running to escape the incoming waves. Running on beyond the high-tide mark, and falling together in the soft sand, tasting the salty spray on each other's lips as we were lost in a warm embrace.

We walked through Seahouses, on to Bamburgh with its beautiful castle. Then, together in the Grace Darling Museum, we marvelled as we relived the short life of that brave young girl.

In the evenings we sat in some corner of a quiet pub whispering, holding hands, all the time discovering.

I told him about beginning my nursing training the following month. I remember feeling pleased that marriage during the three-year training was permitted. At the time it had seemed the obvious, inevitable assumption that we would spend the rest of our lives together.

On two evenings we joined the girls and a group of lads they'd met, and went along to local dances. On each occasion, Graham and I found ourselves breaking away from the crowd, wanting only the company of each other. There, in some darkened corner, all our senses awakened, we swayed together to the throbbing music.

One wet day he borrowed his uncle's old jalopy and took me to Craster, a tiny place famous for its kippers. There, we watched the experts at work as the fish were smoked in the kiln ready for packing.

There were few tourists, and a special air of intimacy hung over the tiny community. We were given a warm welcome and thoughts of settling down and living there washed over me, as we sat with the locals, enjoying a snack lunch in the village pub on the sea-front.

But even as the end of the fortnight loomed nearer, Graham talked only briefly of future plans. He'd be returning to his home in Lancashire shortly after I left, but he'd apply for a job in the Yorkshire town where I lived. It would take time, but, of course, he'd phone and write as soon as I left.

Then, all too soon, it was the last day of my holiday.

At Graham's suggestion, we went over to Holy Island one last time, to say goodbye in the fairy-tale castle where we'd spent our first happy moments together.

Walking through the rooms, we tried to recapture the carefree feeling of our first visit. But somehow, laughter eluded us. We were too conscious of the fact that, next day, I would be leaving and it could be months before we saw one another again.

We were walking hand-in-hand along a sandy cove we had found near the castle, when suddenly we became aware of how late it was.

Graham didn't seem too concerned.

"Come on," he said, "we might just beat the tide if we run."

As we approached the central bridge we could see how high the water was over the causeway.

I felt cold and a little afraid.

"Oh, Graham, what can we do?"

He put his arms around me. He had none of the awkwardness of most of the boys I knew.

"It will be some time before it's safe to cross, Rachel," he said soothingly. "We will have to wait for the tide to go out. Meanwhile, we can stay here."

He led me carefully up into the Refuge; a shelter specially built, high above the water, to harbour fools like us. And there we waited for the tide to turn.

GOING home was a terrible anti-climax. Then began the long wait. By the end of the first week I was convinced the telephone lines to Lancashire were down . . . but on enquiry, the Post Office engineers assured me they were working perfectly.

I waited each morning for the postman. I simply couldn't believe that Graham would desert me like this. Surely something terrible must have happened . . .

I'd never doubted that he would write or phone. And therefore I'd no address . . . there'd seemed no need.

Mum and Dad had tried to warn me, but it was months before I could believe that I would never hear from Graham again.

My parents were shocked when they realised my condition, but they stood by me. I was going to have Graham's child.

The Mother and Baby Home was a warm, caring place, but banished for me any ideas I had of adoption.

When Nicky was born I knew I couldn't part with him. My parents were wonderful, and still are. Without them I could never have kept him.

They wanted me to trace Graham for maintenance, but my pride wouldn't allow it. Dad wanted to set up some form of search but I couldn't let him.

For a long time I expected to see Graham round every corner. I saw him in the glow of a coal fire. I saw him in the foliage of a tree. I saw his face in a cloud formation, in the wallpaper of my bedroom, and in my dreams, always in my dreams.

"Time heals," everyone said. Somehow the memory never did fade. Deep down, beyond the bitterness, there remained a warm glow inside me whenever I thought of him.

ONCE UPON A SUMMER

I suppose it was this feeling which prevented me giving Peter an answer. Dear, steady, reliable Peter.

I lived at home while I did my nursing training, making it possible to see my son, Nicky, every day.

It was in the hospital that I met Peter, working in X-Ray. Very soon our friendship blossomed, but always I felt there was something missing, but I didn't know what. I was perturbed when he asked me to marry him.

"Let me get my finals over first. I don't know. I just don't know."

I was afraid to say yes. I felt if I did, that would abolish the memory of Graham for ever. That I couldn't do, not yet awhile.

Peter had teased me when the results came out. "Hi, Staff Nurse. Now you begin your decision-making."

He knew all about Graham and Nicky, of course, though he didn't know the full details. He'd never asked, perhaps aware that there are things about oneself that must remain private, and for that I loved him all the more.

Then it came to me. I must go back to the Island of Lindisfarne. Perhaps only then could I conquer this thing inside me. If I tried to recapture the magic, just to live again that day when we first met, when it all began.

I told Peter and my parents I needed a weekend away after the strain of my finals. I would stay with a friend in Newcastle. My mother was pleased to have Nicky to herself, and my father lent me the small family car.

SO here I was in search of a lost dream. At times it was almost as if there had never been any such person, that none of it had really happened, but my son is living proof. I've even now stopped asking why. I suppose I'll never know.

I got up from the bench, but before leaving the church, I asked silently for the strength to come to terms with this thing, so that life could go on.

I wanted to go back to the castle, and tread again along the path we'd taken. Then I would go among the lobster pots, find a sheltered spot beside a boathouse, and there I'd sit and remember, drinking some warm coffee from my flask.

Having done all this, perhaps then, I could think more clearly and go to Peter with my answer.

But first I wanted to find a little something, a memento of my love to carry with me always. Some people have lockets or locks of hair. I wanted something to remind me of the island, just something simple.

I'd nearly bought a small print of the castle last year at an auction, but someone else had outbid me.

ONCE UPON A SUMMER

I walked slowly towards the museum shop; I'd seen the sign as I entered the churchyard.

It was a tiny, dark room, with only the daylight from the doorway. I thought it was empty until I became aware of someone sitting in the shadows.

There were a few postcards and guide books, some maps of the island, and remains of local ancient history. I searched for some small thing as a keepsake.

Then I found a tiny model of the castle. It was in one of those small, liquid-filled, glass domes; the kind that create a snowstorm when shaken.

So if my memories ever faded, and if my son should be far away, then I could take out my castle and that way, remember.

I went towards the glass showcase that seemed to serve as a counter, and the figure hidden in the shadows moved forward.

"Eighty pence please, that'll be."

I thought at first the shadows were playing tricks with me. It couldn't be . . . not here.

Then I saw those intense blue eyes that had haunted me over the past years. I was shaking all over . . . I wanted to call out his name. For an instant it was as if the whole world stood still.

"You all right, bonnie lass? Lookin' like you had a fright." His voice was far away, but slowly it was bringing me back to reality.

His tanned face was now fully visible in the beam of light from the doorway. How could I have possibly thought . . . it was only the eyes that held any resemblance . . . the same intense cornflower blue.

I laughed with a great relief.

"I'm all right, thanks. Just mistook you for someone else. Gave me a bit of a shock."

"Ay . . . things ain't always what they seem. There's them that sez the weather up here do strange things to a body." He was wrapping up the small souvenir.

"Somethin' special you lookin' for, lass?" His blue eyes were looking hard at me.

His weather-beaten face showed concern beyond curiosity as he leaned across the counter to get a better look at me. I knew he was not referring to anything he would be able to sell me.

I remembered then, that moment of near-panic . . . that moment when I'd thought he was Graham. But stronger, and still with me, was the tremendous relief on learning that he wasn't.

Somehow, in some way, this man had set me free . . . free from my memory of the past.

"Yes, I suppose I was looking for something special. But thanks to you . . . I think I've found it."

I left him gazing after me, and, clutching my small castle, made my way out into the daylight.

There was something wild and insecure about this island, and I had never noticed it before. Standing in the car park I watched, as the tiny particles of snow mingled with the turrets of the broken castle.

But I knew now I could start building my own castle. Suddenly, more than anything else, I wanted to get back to Peter and my son. □

THE SPANISH HAVE A WORD FOR IT

. . . I only wish I knew what it was, says Sheila Byrne.

IT all began on my way out of church one Sunday morning.

"I'm chairman of a club to foster good relations with people all over the world," my neighbour told me, "and I'm looking for someone to write to a Spaniard who's now living in Bolivia.

"It's a very worthwhile thing," he went on earnestly, "and I'm very much hoping you'll help me out by writing to him."

"But does he know English?" I queried. "I don't know any Spanish."

"Well, no, he doesn't," he admitted, "but he knows a bit of French and I can lend you a few Spanish and French phrase books."

In a weak moment I agreed to try.

That afternoon, when the house was nice and quiet, I got out the phrase books and decided to make a start.

Is it wise to take one's car on the Continent, the phrase books soon made me wonder. "Something," I read, "is wrong with my car, the engine, the gearbox, the lights, the clutch, the brakes, the steering."

After all this came the query, "Can you repair it?" And the reply? "You will need a new — " Car, perhaps?

In the section on "Useful Miscellaneous Phrases" I found many of breathtaking and intriguing interest. For instance, when could it possibly be necessary for a visitor to remark, "I thought I should have got more money for my ducks." Then there were rather more sinister ones, such as "Send for a policeman," and "I wish to consult a good lawyer at once."

A rather sad ending to the holidays, seems to be suggested by, "I have only ten pence left," "Would you have the kindness to direct me to the river?" and "Help."

I decided to grasp at any sentence that seemed to be remotely feasible.

I doubt if the resultant epistle will do more to improve international relations, but no-one can deny that it has a distinction not often found in one's morning post.

Here it is, in translation, of course.

"Dear Sir,

"How do you find yourself today? How do they find themselves at home? I am very well now but I have been in the infirmary.

"My daughter goes to visit her uncle. She must go now. The carriage awaits her. The clock is just about to strike. It is better to be too soon than too late.

"Yesterday it rained much. Tonight it fog. Tomorrow there may be snow. What do you think of the climate in this country?

"What age have you? Twenty-two years? Sixty years? It does not matter. The plough draws the straight furrow.

"I must go now. I must buy a loaf of brown bread. I wish also to post this letter.

"Write to me without delay.

"Respectfully I salute you,

"Your servant and friend."

It wouldn't at all surprise me if the answer was, as the children say, a lemon. I eagerly await it. □

Every Other Weekend

**That was when she said goodbye
to Mummy and for a little while became
Daddy's girl.**

J O couldn't remember — it was so long ago — the day that she and her mother had left the little house in Gosse Way. Granpa was at the door to fetch them away when Jo, tiny then, had run back into the kitchen for her mug, and had knocked it on to the floor. She had run out to the car crying with the two pieces in her hand. Her mother had tried to mend them, but the glue would not hold, so she had tied the halves together with ribbon.

Now the mug, with its Charlie Chimp picture, held pencils and felt pens and was the only ugly thing, cracked and out of place, in the pretty pastel room where Jo slept.

Her books were ranged tidily on the white bookcase that Grandpa had painted; her dolls sat in a row on the little dressing-table. "All Things Bright And Beautiful," the picture that had been Mummy's when she was a girl, hung over the bed. The Magic Roundabout curtains were drawn to keep out the morning sun.

This Saturday morning, Jo woke as she always did — suddenly and completely. She saw the dolls on the dressing-table, neatly dressed for the weekend, and her case by the door, ready packed.

EVERY OTHER WEEKEND

Her shiny recorder was on the chair by her bed. Her mother had told her with a little frown, "You must take care of it; it's very kind of Granny to buy it for you."

And her grandmother, pursing up her lips and frowning too, had said: "We can afford it."

Jo practised that frown, being her grandmother; then practised frowning the way that her mother did, anxious and sad.

She could hear the grown-ups downstairs moving quietly so as not to wake her. Granpa would be cleaning the shoes, and Granny getting the breakfast.

Her mother had to go to the shops on Saturday mornings. Granpa had told her, "You don't have to go out to work at all," but Jo's mother had said, "I like it at the flower shop. The people are so very nice" — nice people were important to Jo's mother — "and I must have something to do."

Jo played a few notes on the recorder — she was a tap dripping, ping, ping, poing! Like the tap dripping on to the plastic washing-up bowl in Daddy's kitchen.

She blew again — liquid notes. "Raindrops Keep Falling On My Head." That was difficult. Her father had told her, "You have to *be* what you are playing. Your fingers have to *be* the raindrops — and your head has to be a little aloof, watching and criticising your fingers."

Jo had thought that was funny; she had said: "A cat is aloof, a critical cat." She remembered how she and Daddy had laughed.

She tried a few notes of the teasing, tiptoeing melody that her father had taught her on the half-size violin . . .

Then she remembered that she was a tap dripping, just in time, as her mother opened the bedroom door and peeped in. "There's a good girl, practising. But now you must get up. Granpa will be ready to take you at nine."

Jo put the recorder back on the chair. "I don't want to go. There'll be nothing to do."

"Darling, please. Don't start that again." Her mother's face crumpled.

Jo lay stiffly under the blankets.

"Get up, darling," her mother pleaded. "I've packed your blue nightie. And the dolls can go in their basket. Take the recorder. Have you told Daddy you joined the beginners' class at school? You never tell me what he says . . . I wonder he doesn't teach you a few tunes when you stay with him."

Rigid, Jo watched her mother pack the recorder on top of the nightdress. "Come along, darling, please."

"I shall scream."

"There's yoghurt for breakfast. With nuts."

She always had yoghurt and nuts for a breakfast treat before the Every-Other-Weekends.

"I had bad dreams in the night. I woke up and I — "

"You slept very well." Her mother spoke sharply, then crumpled again. "Please darling, get up, mustn't keep Grandpa waiting."

"I shall be sick in the car." Then Jo thought of the yoghurt and nuts. "You'll have to make me get up."

Thankfully, for this was the end of Stage One, her mother pulled back the bedclothes, sat her up, began to dress her like a baby. "Take your vitamins at bedtime; Daddy forgets."

"Yes, Mummy," Jo said meekly, sad and big eyed. "He always forgets. Thinking of his own things to do."

They were silent, her mother brushing Jo's hair, holding her. "Daddy's hair is thick. Does he remember to brush it? Does he remember . . . does he keep the house clean?"

Jo considered, choosing from so many answers — clean wasn't the word you thought of for Daddy, there were so many better words. She sighed, shaking her head, using her mother's little frown. "Not very tidy."

"Does anyone come in to clean? But I suppose if he's not working full-time. If only he could have had a regular job — "

"There's Jenny, of course," Jo said casually.

Her mother let go of her, and Jo nearly fell off the bed.

"Who's Jenny?"

"Oh — just Jenny." Jo refused to pursue her. She didn't want to tell her mother anything about her weekends with her father, although her mind was full of her father's house, cold and untidy.

Funny to think that she and Mummy had lived there once with Daddy — he had shown her the marks in the hall where her pram had scraped the wallpaper, and there was a bottle of perfume still on the bathroom shelf.

"Shall I take it home to Mummy?" she had asked, before Daddy had put it away, out of sight, in the bathroom cabinet.

Sighing deeply, Jo stood while her mother fastened her sandals. She knew that all weekend, her mother would be thinking of her, worrying. As she always did Every-Other-Weekend.

In the car, Jo told her grandfather, "I feel sick. When we get to the corner by Mrs Smith's shop I shall cry."

He was old. "You must be a good little girl, like your mother was. She was such a good little thing, always. When she got married we missed her so much."

"I want to be good. But I hate leaving you, Granpa."

Watching the traffic, he patted her knee with one hand. "You are only away for the weekend, dear. We've promised your father to bring you every other weekend. Promises have to be kept."

"Yes, Granpa." She said that good-as-gold; then wriggled and looked behind her. Her case lay on the back seat, the recorder hidden under her nightie. "Granpa! The dolls' basket! It's got left behind!"

O N her father's doorstep she held her little case tightly, turning a long trembly look towards Granpa, who waited uncomfortably at the gate.

EVERY OTHER WEEKEND

Why she acted like this she had no idea; only — it was exciting, and she must, somehow, keep the two halves of her life apart.

"I'll bring the dolls over — " he offered.

"No, don't, Granpa. Don't come, don't — "

But already the door was open, and her father was saying, "Thanks for bringing her, Mr Blakey."

Then she was inside, and he held her; she had forgotten her grandfather already. She clung to her father in the cold hall, sniffing the smell of the house. "Is it kippers? Or onions? Or something burning? It's burnt vegetable soup, isn't it?"

"It's the cake I made. I thought it couldn't be that hard. In the war, I remember my mother used custard powder and vinegar when we didn't have eggs. I'm sure she used vinegar."

"Oh, Daddy!"

"Leave your case here. I'm terribly busy. I've got a man coming at ten, and Mrs Barnaby at eleven, and a fat little boy after that who squeaks like a rat. What will you do?"

The house smelled — kind of funny. And it was cold. The sink would be full of dishes. But the house held out its arms, welcomingly. "Is Teddy upstairs?"

"He's on top of the fridge. He thinks he knows more about cooking than I do, but he doesn't. Where are the dolls?

"What will you do? You could play next door with Mrs Waller's Elisabeth; she asked when you were coming. I give lessons every Saturday now. I like it — it helps me with my own work."

"I'll wash up," Jo decided. "Will Jenny be coming?"

In the kitchen she nodded to Teddy, high on the fridge. There were damp fish fingers on the table among the drawing paper, charcoal and paint.

Her father always pinned up her drawings on the cork notice board — it was odd to think that Granpa had made that board for the wall long ago when Mummy and Daddy were first married, before Jo was born. Odd to think that Mummy had done the careful lettering: THINGS TO REMEMBER.

Daddy had pinned up the portrait of an "Aloof Critical Cat" — the one they had been laughing about last Every-Other- Weekend.

She put on a torn apron — this was her kitchen. Different from Granny's. And Mummy hadn't a kitchen of her own at all.

The sink was certainly full of dirty dishes, and the burnt cake tin, and the sharp knife on which she had once cut herself.

She stood on tiptoe, dabbling the plates in the water.

People are like plates, she thought, juggled up in the air: Mummy and Daddy and Granny and Granpa, juggled up in the air, and you must keep them separate or else they will smash all to pieces, with nasty sharp edges . . .

She soon tired of dishwashing and went upstairs to unpack her suitcase. She hid the shiny recorder under her spare jeans; she didn't want to tell her father about the beginners' class, though it would

Continued on page 142.

"Ain't I Got Style"

by JEAN WILLIS

Well, *I* think I have. It's just a pity my taste is always guaranteed to raise a highbrow's eyebrows!

I SOMETIMES wonder if there can be anyone living in this world who equals me for lack of taste.

I don't mean taste in the sense of savouring flavours — what I mean is, I seem to have an instinctive preference for the things which always seem to horrify more discriminating people.

It is beyond me, for example, why a colour scheme I regard as an atrocity sends others into raptures of enthusiasm, whilst my choice invariably produces an agonised expression.

I have had to learn to live with the fact that what I like is usually somewhat different to other people's ideas of good taste.

But I still claim it was purely coincidental that my husband's bout of insomnia started after he let me have a free hand in the redecoration of our bedroom.

I am sure it has nothing to do with the yellow stars on the midnight blue ceiling, the pink striped wallpaper and the red carpet. I can't see what he is complaining about. I like it. It's cheerful!

There are those who believe I have good dress sense. Any compliments in this direction give me the sort of pangs of conscience I had as a schoolgirl when I had cribbed answers. The truth of the matter is, I dare not choose my own clothes unadvised.

The genius behind my wardrobe is, in fact, my seven-year-old son. He may not enjoy shopping for my clothes, but he is an expert at it.

When I am trying on garments, just one glance at his face is more informative than an hour of posturing before a mirror.

Sometimes I think I am alone in my plebeian tastes, particularly in such things as art, music and entertainments. But surely not. After all, I can't believe they make Westerns purely for me, yet rarely do I hear anyone else confess to liking them.

I get enormous enjoyment from watching the arrows fly and the baddies biting the dust, and since they continue to produce Westerns on a commercial basis, I think many people speak with forked tongue!

I am also comforted by the fact that whilst I obviously do not appreciate many things to their full depth, I do at least *enjoy* them.

In my deep-freeze, fish fingers nestle close to the smoked salmon. Books by famous authors rub shoulders in my bookcase with paperbacks showing an inevitable pallid maiden gazing up cow-eyed at a dashingly-handsome young man. And my record collection is composed of folk music, operatic arias, concertos, jazz and large helpings of Mantovani.

My husband claims that anyone walking into our house can tell in minutes that I am a real philistine. However, he does admit that on one occasion in my life I did display impeccable taste and unimpeachable judgment. I married him! □

Continued from page 140.

amuse him to hear about the teacher, Miss Marchant.

But that belonged to her other world, the one in which she went to school and learned her notes and was mostly a quiet, good child.

Downstairs she heard the scrape and bowing of her father's pupils; she wondered if he ever let *them* play the pieces that he wrote.

At Granny's on Saturdays there would be savoury mince or hot sausages. Her father's fish fingers were soggy.

"Did you tell Mummy?" he asked her. "About my two jobs? I work three days a week at St Edmund's and two days at the Tech. as well as my Saturday lessons. That's regular work, isn't it?"

She nodded, not listening, wiping the dripping ketchup bottle with her fingertip.

"I can give you pocket money — you must tell your grandfather that, and not take any from him. I enjoy teaching and what's more it helps me with my own work, writing."

"How much pocket money, Daddy?" But she wasn't very interested.

"You *will* tell Mummy — don't forget, will you, Jo?"

AFTER lunch the child from next door came in, so they pushed aside the dishes and Jo fetched the small violin that her father was teaching them to play, and his three recorders, treble, alto and bass.

All the rooms were full of papers and music; upstairs in the back bedroom he now kept his class-teaching things — this week a stack of percussion instruments — and a pile of records.

"These are Negro songs," he told them. "Some sad, some very lively. I'll put on a record and you two can join in with the recorders when you are ready . . . This is the first one. 'Walking In Jerusalem Just Like John'. Now try to keep time."

They had been playing for some time, enjoying themselves and making a great deal of noise, when the front doorbell rang. . .

"Don't stop," Jo said. "I'll go down; it's probably Jenny."

For a moment she didn't recognise the figure standing on the doorstep holding the basket of dolls. Didn't recognise her, because she belonged so definitely to that other world.

"I thought it was Jenny. *You* never come here. Never, never, never."

Her mother stood, looking at her. "Your granpa couldn't get the car started. I was afraid you wouldn't settle without the dolls, so I came on the bus."

The dolls meant nothing to Jo, here, in her father's house.

Her mother looked past her into the chill angular hall. Upstairs Elisabeth was shaking a tambourine, and her father's voice was still singing.

Jo stood frozen, unable to move. Her two worlds were meeting, two worlds with the jagged crack between them, one world cracked apart, so that there was one home in Granny's house and another home here Every-Other-Weekend.

"I thought you were Jenny," she repeated coldly, trembling.

Her mother stepped past her gently, carrying the dolls. "It's a very long time — since I've been here," she said slowly.

Jo moved to stand defensively at the foot of the stairs. Her father had put on another record, and he and Elisabeth were singing loudly, "Ring On Dem Bells . . ."

How little her mother seemed, looking anxiously upward.

Then the bedroom door opened and her father called: "Who is it? Has Jenny come?" He came to the top of the stairs and stopped short. "Rose!"

Jo had never seen him look like that before. She stood at the foot of the stairs, between them.

"I only came — " her mother began to explain.

"Rose," he said again, gently, wonderingly, and began to come downstairs.

Her mother's eyes were fixed on his. Jo stood, rooted, and her father reached the bottom step and put his hands on her shoulders, firmly moving her aside.

"You came, Rose," he said, sounding as if he didn't believe it. He took the doll's basket from her and put it down, so that he could hold both her hands, and suddenly he was smiling, and so was Jo's mother, and there were tears in her eyes.

"Daddy," Jo said loudly, but they weren't listening to her. Her mother's hands were on his shoulders, and she was saying, "There's just one thing. Who's Jenny?"

"Jenny?" Her father was impatient. "She's the kid up the road — she comes in to clean round when she needs extra pocket money . . ."

The half-open front door crashed back on its hinges. "Sorry I'm late — oh, sorry!" Jenny paused in the act of taking off her blazer and looked doubtfully at Jo's mother, and then at Jo.

"This is Jenny," Jo's father said, and Jo's mother turned in his arms to look. "See for yourself."

"I see. Hello, Jenny. Well — look — " She turned back. "I have to go — I only brought Jo's dolls . . ."

Jo shook her head at Jenny, and the big girl nodded and put her blazer back on.

Jo's parents didn't hear the front door close behind Jenny.

"At least have some tea," her father was saying. "There was meant to be cake. You've never come before. You've never been back — " There was no barrier between them now.

Jo slipped away into the kitchen, and began to fill the kettle.

A cup of tea — that was what grown-ups always expected. She settled the kettle on the stove and looked for clean cups among the jostle of dishes and charcoal.

She listened. Upstairs Elisabeth and the record player played on, but there was no sound from the hall.

She was tired of being busy alone in the kitchen. Her two worlds were coming together; her one cracked world was mending. □

144

Complete Story By **SUSAN SALLIS**

THE PATIENT IN WARD SIX

**All the old lady could offer her
were a few kind words
— and the certainty that someone
was listening . . .**

A LICE opened the door of the single ward attached to Ward 6 and slipped quietly inside. The curtains were drawn and in the dim light she could see the girl lying in bed, her hair sticky around her head, her hands tucked into the covers just as Sister must have left her after the morning rounds.

Alice came closer and the girl's wide brown eyes, fixed unseeingly on the ceiling, flickered slightly.

K

"It's all right, dear," Alice said softly. "I've just come to clean your room for you. Don't worry, Sister told me you must be quiet so I haven't got the polisher. I'm not very keen on it myself actually. I'd rather manage the old-fashioned way. Spit and polish. Elbow grease." She smiled cheerfully at the brown eyes but they did not move again or make any attempt to focus on her.

"Take Mrs Jenner," Alice continued. "Now you'll have had her cleaning over the weekend, I expect, because I'm only here weekdays — not that I'd mind coming in at weekends at all. Quite the opposite. I love my work and seeing all of you. It's such company, you see. But they only let me work so many hours a week now. Daft, isn't it? When I've been used to working a twelve-and fourteen-hour day all my life."

She laughed, and rubbed at the taps in the washbasin till they gleamed. "Now where was I? Yes, Mrs Jenner. She loves the polisher. She says it saves her talking or listening to anyone. Can you understand it? That's the part of the job I love."

She rinsed the basin thoroughly, then moved to the locker.

"There's some lovely grapes here, dear. Why don't you try one? Sister says you haven't had any breakfast, or supper last night, and I don't suppose you'd eaten much before you were brought in." She leaned over the bed. Not a muscle moved in the still, staring face. But Alice smiled.

"Later on perhaps, eh? I expect your husband brought them in. Maybe he can persuade you to have a few." The eyes seemed to widen still more.

Alice patted the covers.

"Now don't fret, dear. If I've said anything out of place, just forget it. I'm only the cleaner, no-one takes any notice of old Alice." She smiled again. "That's my name, Alice. I don't stand on ceremony like Mrs Jenner. Everyone calls me Alice." She straightened her back briskly. "I'll start on the floor now. Give me a call if you want anything. It's Alice, remember."

She fetched her kneeler out of her box and started by the window. "Yes, like I was saying, this is a much better way of doing the floors. We wouldn't have knees if we weren't intended to kneel on them, would we?" She gave a chuckle and pushed herself back a yard or two.

"'Course, what I like about these kneelers is you can skate around on them like they were a sledge! Gives that bit of extra shine, too." She demonstrated, and wondered whether she imagined that the white face on the bed turned fractionally to watch her.

"Reminds me of my Lizzie. We only had the one girl, my husband and me. Lizzie. She loved to help me do the work. I never had any difficulty amusing her. Give her a duster and she'd be happy for hours. We used to tie rags round our feet and skate up and down the passage till the lino was like glass. What a laugh we had! My husband used to say that when I stopped laughing the world would come to an end!"

Alice sat back on her heels and surveyed her work critically.

"'Course, when we lost our Lizzie the world nearly did come to an end for a bit. Diptheria it was. People still died of it in those days and she was only six so she didn't have much strength to fight it off."

She sighed sharply and continued cleaning with extra energy. "But the war was on and there was plenty to do. I looked after a barrage balloon — would you believe it? A great lumbering thing it was, stuck up there by the aircraft factory. I called it Gladys because it reminded me of my Auntie Glad who was always puffing and overweight. That got me laughing again."

Alice took a last rub around the skirting board and stood up creakily. "That's better. The place looks really nice now. Ready for visiting time this afternoon."

She tidied up her dusters, picked up her box and went to the bed. "I'll see you again tomorrow morning. And perhaps you'll have had something to eat then, eh?" The brown eyes stared at the ceiling.

"It sounds silly," Alice continued, "but you'll feel much better when you've had something to eat." She patted the covers again. "I ought to call you something, oughtn't I? What's your name?"

No answer came and she went to the bottom of the bed and looked at the chart. "Well, I'm blowed. Elizabeth. Mrs Elizabeth Garnet." She shook her head. "Isn't that a coincidence? Not that you're anything like my Lizzie. She'd be forty now, and you — you're only twenty-eight. But still, it's nice, that.

"It's like I used to say to my Arnie when he got low and depressed — life's got to go on — nothing can stop it, so we've got to make the best of it." She chuckled. "I think he believed me right at the end because he didn't used to get so angry — so bitter. D'you know, he even told me that maybe I wasn't as daft as I sounded!"

Her voice softened. "Why don't you close your eyes now, dear, and have a little nap till they bring in your lunch?"

She waited, but Elizabeth Garnet continued to stare at the ceiling.

"Go on, dear. Close your eyes. Don't be frightened to go to sleep. Think of me skidding around on my old kneeler and you'll have happy dreams."

The eyes flickered and then closed. Alice held her breath and tiptoed to the door. It was the men's ward now and the electric polisher and everyone calling, "Hello, Alice!"

She would enjoy that. But it had been nice to be quiet for a bit. Nice to have a proper chat.

THE next morning, Nurse Deakin came out of Mrs Garnet's single ward frowning.

"Hello, Alice." She smiled, as Alice showed her the Get Well card she brought. "You're going in to Mrs Garnet now, are you? No polisher, mind."

Alice shook her head. "How is she this morning, Nurse? Did she have any breakfast?"

THE PATIENT IN WARD SIX

"No." The worried frown returned. "I thought she might be on the mend yesterday too. She had some soup at lunch-time and let me comb her hair. But after visiting time she was as bad as ever. It's almost like a coma."

Alice nodded. "Reminds me of my old mum when she had her stroke. Is it something like that?"

"Oh, no. It's psychosomatic . . . you wouldn't understand, Alice. She was driving the family car — crashed it — her son was killed. She seemed to get over it, then a week ago she lost the use of her legs. Only it's all in her mind."

"Well, there's Doctor Henry — he's the one should see her — "

"Both our psychiatrists have seen her. She refuses to speak. Or look at them."

"Her husband then."

"She won't speak to him. She's always a lot worse after he's been."

"So she's just lying there on her own. Why doesn't someone just go in and *talk* to her?"

"Oh, Alice . . . we do, of course, but she can't hear, you see. She's cut herself off from all human contact. It's guilt . . . you wouldn't understand, Alice."

"Maybe I would and maybe I wouldn't," Alice said darkly. "All I know is when my mum got a bit better after her stroke she said to me — 'I heard every word you said to me, Alice, so you needn't think I've missed anything while I've been ill!' And *she* used to lie there hour after hour, day in and day out, just staring and never speaking a word!"

Nurse Deakin's voice was impatient. "Well, Mrs Garnet hasn't had a stroke so it's rather different. She thinks it's her fault her little boy is dead and that her husband is blaming her. She can't bear it so she's shut herself away where she can't hear or see anything. And I've got work to do if you haven't!"

Alice watched her go then picked up her box of polish and dusters and went in to Mrs Garnet's room.

"Good morning, dear," she said softly but cheerfully. "It's Alice. Remember me? I've come to clean your room again."

The brown eyes stared at the ceiling but the tight mouth seemed to relax just a little.

Alice smiled. "That's better. I was glad to hear you had a drop of soup yesterday. I'm very partial to some soup myself."

She tightened the belt of her nylon overall and went to the basin.

"Of course, we always used to make our own, you know. Not like these packets and tins you get nowadays. Pea soup. That was my favourite.

"Lizzie loved it. That's my little girl who died — d'you remember I told you about her? She loved pea soup. And, d'you know — " she looked steadily at the bed " — my Arnie wouldn't touch it after Lizzie died."

Elizabeth Garnet's facial muscles contracted slightly as if with a spasm of pain.

"He said it reminded him of her! As if that was something awful. I said to him straight — 'I should hope it does, Arnie — I should hope everything reminds you of our Lizzie. Surely you don't want to forget her,' I said."

Very slowly the head on the pillow turned and Alice felt the brown eyes on her.

"He said he was surprised I could bear to be reminded of her because he couldn't. It hurt too much, he said." Alice smiled down at the white face beneath her as if they were sharing a secret together. "I told him straight. I told him he should be glad it hurt. Because if it didn't hurt it would be as if our Lizzie hadn't been with us at all. It would be as if we hadn't had those six lovely years with her. I told him we'd get used to the pain."

She went across and fetched her kneeler. "Well, you get used to anything in time, don't you? You remember the good times. The funny times. Like skating down our passage hall with dusters on our feet." She chuckled reminiscently. "Better than any electric polisher. I'll have to remember to tell Mrs Jenner that if I see her tonight. It'll make her laugh. She's very shy and retiring is Mrs Jenner — that's why she likes the electric polisher, because she can sort of hide behind it."

Alice finished her work and as she stood up again she saw that Mrs Garnet's eyes were closed and her mouth relaxed in a half-smile. Alice smiled to herself, well satisfied, and packed her dusters away, already planning how she would tell Mr Hennessy in the men's ward that Nurse Deakin did not have a permanent boyfriend.

A WEEK later Elizabeth Garnet was taking small amounts of food but still refused obstinately to speak to anyone.

Her dark eyes followed Alice around the room faithfully each morning and once when Alice's rough hand patted the coverlet she seized it and looked at it closely.

And when Alice said, "It's a pity you haven't got your mother to come and see you. You need your mother now, I reckon," a tear trickled down the pale cheek.

Alice tried to comfort her. "That's right, dear — let them come. Have a good cry." But Elizabeth Garnet fell back on her pillows, exhausted, her eyes going back to the ceiling.

The next day, Alice cleaned the windows. "I don't mind doing windows. I was always doing them at one time and I suppose I got used to it."

THE PATIENT IN WARD SIX

She smiled at the bed where Elizabeth was propped up, some knitting lying idly on the sheet in front of her. "Lizzie was a devil for drawing on the windows. She'd spit on her finger and do all her letters — she could do the alphabet before she went to school, you know."

She rubbed away proudly, and behind her Elizabeth Garnet nodded too. Alice saw the nodding head reflected in her window pane and her smile widened. "That's the sort of thing I want you . . . " Her voice died and she corrected herself hastily. "That's the sort of thing I wanted Arnie to remember. I told him so often. But all he'd do was talk about the pain of it. And how if he'd had a decent job we could have afforded to get the doctor in sooner, how he felt responsible . . ."

There was a faint sound from behind her but she chose to ignore it.

"I used to say," she went on firmly, " 'If you go on like this you'll make me as bad as yourself.' I threatened to take up with another bloke — " she chuckled richly " — not that anyone would have had me!

"And then, d'you know what happened? I got ill myself. Got pneumonia! Not too bad, but bad enough for Arnie to have to pull himself together and nurse me. It frightened him to death and he was a different man by the time I was well again."

She came over to the bed, folding her cloth carefully. "Well, that's that for today, dear. I see you passed on your grapes to Mrs Barnes up the hall. That was kind of you but I shouldn't tell your husband. Let him think you've eaten them. And if he brings in some more you ought to try to have them yourself."

She picked up the knitting. "Let me guess . . . socks. Couldn't be much else on four needles, could it? I'm sure your husband will like them, and if you work hard you'll have this one finished by the time I see you again on Monday."

She walked to the door. "We've got to keep going, dear. Whether it's polishing windows or knitting, we've got to keep going."

Elizabeth Garnett looked at her knitting. Slowly, she picked it up and began.

O N Saturday afternoon, Alice left the small room where she lived alone and went into town to do her weekly shopping. She wasn't feeling well and the thought of being ill with no-one to call and see her dimmed her usual cheerfulness.

She hurried out of the pedestrian shopping precinct to catch an early bus and, forgetting she had left the traffic-free zone, stepped straight out into the road . . .

There was a lot of pain and confusion. It began to rain, a light summer shower which made her shiver, then she was constricted by blankets. Then young Dr Carr from Casualty was saying, "Well, if it isn't our Alice. What have you been doing to yourself — you're not fit to be let loose . . . " And a hypodermic slid into her arm.

Alice opened her eyes to the unmistakable smell of Sunday morning. Bacon and porridge and tea, against the antiseptic and clean linen smells. She moved each limb cautiously. She ached but nothing seemed broken. She was propped up on her pillows; so was everyone else. And a rank of oxygen canisters was marshalled by the door. She was in the chest ward.

An unfamiliar nurse came over with some tea. "You don't mind too much being kept in for a few days, Alice? You had a nasty shock, and with your history we were scared of pneumonia."

"Mind? I don't mind at all." Alice smiled and accepted the tea gratefully. "All the people I like best are in here, why should I mind being with them?"

She settled back to enjoy herself. The lady in the opposite bed was smiling at her already. It couldn't have worked out better. She would be fit enough to get up tomorrow and do Mrs Garnet's room for her as usual.

And she was escaping the weekend. Weekends were lonely times, when if she wasn't very careful all her happy memories became sad and it was as if she looked down on herself from a great height and saw a solitary old woman with nothing to show for her life. And that wasn't good.

She slept and woke and wanted to sleep again. One of the students listened to her chest and she saw that the nurses were taking round the bed-time drinks. She couldn't understand what had happened to the day.

She woke several times in the night to try to move the heavy weight from her chest. The royal-blue uniform of a Sister seemed always by her bed and she tried to smile at her but her mouth was dry and cracking.

It was daylight.

"Lizzie," she whispered. "Must see Lizzie."

"She's delirious," she heard Sister say in a low voice. "Fetch the oxygen, Nurse — "

"Must go skating," Alice said with the last of her breath. "It's time to go skating."

Nurse's smile was bright and artificial. "We can't go skating on a nice day like this, can we, Alice?" She presented the oxygen mask. "Come along, dear. You'll feel better after you've had some of this."

Alice breathed deeply. It was so frustrating that she couldn't make them understand.

Day became night again. It was a long night. She was tired and couldn't sleep. When daylight paled the windows she wondered whether she was going to die. Death did not frighten her but that she should die without anyone special near her . . . not that it mattered. Keep going, Alice. Keep smiling.

"Someone to see you, dear!" Sister's face came close to hers as if they all thought she was going deaf. The sun shone across the bed brightly so it must be afternoon. Someone sat down and leaned forward. It was Mrs Jenner.

THE PATIENT IN WARD SIX

Alice's mouth was too dry to smile and she turned her head away, not wanting Mrs Jenner to see her so miserable.

"You'll soon be better, Alice. Soon back to work I shouldn't wonder. Mr Hennessy sends his love and to tell you Nurse Deakin winked at him on Sunday."

Alice moved her stiff tongue. "Lizzie . . . " she whispered. "Lizzie . . . "

She heard Sister's voice. "That's her daughter, I believe. She's wandering again, I'm afraid."

Mrs Jenner came closer. "Listen, Alice, I wanted to tell you . . . listen if you can. You know you told me about skidding around on your kneeler when you polished the floors? Well, I got to thinking.

And now when I use the electric polisher, I pretend I'm dancing. With someone very handsome. What do you think of that?"

Sister sounded astonished. "Well, look at that! I do believe she's laughing! I wonder what she's thinking about now?"

"Maybe she heard me," Mrs Jenner said. "Anyway I wanted to tell her that. It would please her. She was always trying to make me have a bit of fun."

"Lizzie . . . Lizzie . . . " Alice whispered.

"Let her rest now, Mrs Jenner," Sister said. "We mustn't tire her out."

THE sun lay in orange bars on the floor. It was evening. Alice closed her eyes because she couldn't keep them open any longer.

People spoke to her; not a proper conversation; small encouraging snippets. "Just a sip of water, Alice . . . " "Five minutes with the mask again, Alice . . . " then, "It's no good, she can't hear."

She wanted to open her eyes and tell them sharply that of course she could hear every word they said. She just couldn't answer, that was all.

She must have slept again. She became conscious of the voice when it was halfway through a sentence and had obviously introduced itself. Not that she needed any introductions.

" . . . and you just kept talking, d'you remember? Even though I never answered you, you just kept talking, Alice. And that's why I'm sitting here chatting away and not bothered because you don't open your eyes. I know you can hear me.

"I'm going to sit here and talk to you and say the same things over and over again . . . I'm not going to stop, Alice. Because I'm your

152

contact with life, just as you were mine. If you hadn't talked to me and kept in contact, I think I would have died."

The voice faltered for an instant and then went on strongly. "You've made me get out of bed, Alice, and come to see you. Just as you made your Arnie stir himself all those years ago when you had your first bout of pneumonia. But before that . . . when you left on Friday . . . I did lots of knitting, Alice. I turned the heel of that first sock. And when John came to visit me — John's my husband — I told him the sock was for him. And he cried. And I cried, too."

Alice felt her hand taken and pressed hard. "It's good to cry together, Alice, isn't it? It's the first step towards laughing together. We shall do that soon, Alice. I promise you. When we remember some of the funny things Simon used to do — he used to draw on the window, too. Just like your Lizzie. Perhaps all children do it . . . and he was six too . . . like Lizzie."

The hand tightened, drawing Alice towards it. "I want to tell you, Alice — it might be a long time since anyone told you this . . . I want you to know. It's very important to me, Alice. In that week when you talked to me, you became very important to me, Alice. Your face . . . your hands . . . everything about you . . . you are so beautiful. That's what I want you to know, Alice. You are beautiful. Can you understand that?"

Alice opened her parched lips with difficulty, but she could not open her eyes.

"Lizzie . . . " she murmured.

"Yes," the voice said softly. "It's Lizzie. It's Lizzie . . . "

Elizabeth Garnet laid the hand carefully on the coverlet and stood up. Sister listened in vain with her stethoscope.

"I'm afraid she couldn't hear you, Mrs Garnet. She was in a coma at the end."

Elizabeth Garnet looked down at Alice and smiled. "She heard me," she said confidently. "She heard every word. She called me by my name, didn't you hear her?"

Sister shook her head. "That was her daughter's name, too, I'm afraid. She thought — "

Elizabeth's smile grew. "She thought I was her child? Maybe I was in a way. She came to me when I needed a mother most. And she put me straight — like mothers do."

She went through the screens and joined the man waiting for her anxiously outside the ward.

"Liz — are you all right? You're not strong enough — you've been in there two hours."

"I'm all right, John. I'm coming home now, my dear." She turned and looked back. Just once. "There's a lot to be done."

"But, darling, what on earth did you find to say in there? You've hardly spoken a word for ages, yet I could hear your voice the whole time."

Elizabeth smiled. "I was chatting. That's all. Alice and I . . . we enjoy a quiet chat." □

OUR MAIRI

She'd had a hard life — and a sad one — but, finally, the sun
shone on the wee tinker lass, just as we'd
always hoped it would . . .

By GIDEON SCOTT MAY

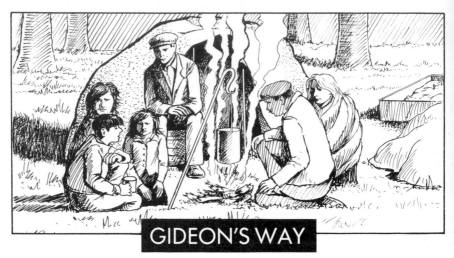

GIDEON'S WAY

THE Fraternity, as tinkers are
sometimes termed, are
part and parcel of the
Scottish Highlands.

One of the most colourful
characters, Your Honour,
christened himself with his mode of
address. These two opening words
from him would quickly elevate
anyone to a position ranking with
the highest in the land.

I always considered his accolade
worth every penny of the 50 he
required to purchase "a cup of
tea." I knew which brew Your
Honour invariably had in mind — a
golden glass of whisky, which he
would croon over in the Gaelic as
he sipped.

It was said that Crafty Kate, the
uncrowned queen of The Fraternity,

was his common-law wife, but no-
one was sure. One day, Kate
called at Croft Douglas and tried to
sell me a pair of solid silver
candlesticks.

"Where on earth did you get
these?" I gasped.

"Oh," she answered airily, "they
were in the old church down the
glen. The door was open and
nobody was looking after
anything."

"Kate," I said severely, "the Lord
will probably strike you dead with
lightning for doing this."

"Oh no," she cried. "I'm feart o'
lightning."

"Then you must put back those
holy holders of light where you
found them," I said. "Or it won't
be lightning that will strike you, but

a thunderbolt from on high!"

Whereupon Kate clutched the candlesticks with one hand, lifted her tattered skirt with the other and ran like the wind to make amends.

Kate had a daughter whose christening was a sprinkling of water from a spring on the side of Schiehallion, after which she answered to the name of Mairi.

Mairi, now a well-grown teenager, went her own independent way and, one spring morning when the birds were mating and marking their territories with a song, Mairi was found about to have a baby in a tinker's tent by the roadside. A police car picked her up and raced to the cottage hospital where a friend of ours, Flora, had just produced a little boy.

That evening, during the visiting hour, we were at Flora's bedside. Her locker was ablaze with a huge bunch of golden daffodils. As we greeted her, she put her fingers to her lips, saying softly, "Please talk in whispers. Mairi is asleep."

I LOOKED across to the next bed. A mane of black hair, with the gloss of a raven's wing, flowed across the pillow sweeping away from a finely-chiselled face.

"Nobody has been in to see her," Flora whispered in worried tones. "And I know she would be too proud to share my flowers."

I knew exactly what Flora meant and, on the way home, left an order with Macpherson's, the florist, for a bunch of flowers to be sent to Mairi.

Mairi was awake on our next visit and the bunch of red roses by her bedside brought a pleasurable bloom to her cheeks.

The winter that followed was a merciless one and news came to me that Mairi's little one had got caught in its chilly claws and died.

In the springtime I heard there had been a tinker's wedding and that Mairi had married The Quiet One.

Her husband was reputed to have the cleverest pair of hands in the Highlands and I had seen some of his willow-weaving work and delicate horn carvings.

The swallows came and went for six summers when, one day, there came a tiny tap at the door and I found a little girl standing on the step.

She held out a hand-woven basket full of spoons which, she solemnly assured me, were carved from the horns of a Highland bull, haltingly adding," . . . and Mother says to leave the pricing of them to yourself."

As the little girl left, I followed her around the end of the house. Her mother was waiting there. It was Mairi.

At the roadside I could see a gaily-painted caravan bedecked with baskets with hazel sticks. It was drawn by a skewbald pony and, standing at its head, The Quiet One.

I rejoiced for Mairi, who not only had that lovely little girl to compensate for her loss, but was now the proud partner in what, I was sure, would be a thriving business.

From my sporran, I removed a five-shilling piece, given to me by a gipsy who prophesied that I would never want for money as long as I had it.

I felt that here was someone who needed it more than I did, and I pressed it into Mairi's hand.

Not wishing to hurt the pride in her new-found independence, I hastily stuttered, "It's for . . . it's for good luck, Mairi."

She turned around. Her smile was a sunbeam filtering through the fingers of a morning mist.

"Then I will never, ever spend it," she said. □

A House Or A Home

. . . Wise men have tried to define the difference. Cathy learned it in the most unexpected way . . .

CATHY walked along the tree-lined lane. It was very warm and the trees hung listless in the humid afternoon . . .

It was a nice place. She'd thought so from the moment Peter had brought her to see the house.

"It's got promise, Cath," he'd said as he walked with her up the grassy track.

It had been spring and several of the trees were cherry. Candyfloss

157

blossom drifted gently down as they passed under the rioting bloom.

"Needs a lot doing, of course — the house is getting on a bit. Still, we can do it in stages. Main thing is to get a home of our own. Much better to have a house when the baby arrives. He'll need his own room."

She hadn't replied. She was sad at the prospect of leaving the flat.

The flat was special. They'd begun married life there. Decorated it beautifully. Everyone said so. It had character.

It wasn't practical, of course. Deep down she knew Peter was right to want to buy a place of their own, but she couldn't become enthusiastic about house-hunting.

After much discussion they'd bought the house — such a long time ago now, it seemed. Now she was making her way towards it for the first time on her own.

She stopped by the gate that was peeling its paint and looked at the house.

It had a sad, abandoned air. Almost of being unloved.

"We started our married life here, dear," the previous owner had confided to Cathy. "There's been good times under this roof and bad. Still, you wouldn't expect it any other way, would you?"

Cathy had nodded and looked round at the dark-brown paint and old-fashioned wallpaper. She'd thought longingly of the white walls of the flat and her pretty curtains. So light and bright they'd made the flat. Now . . .

She wondered if Peter realised just how much work he was taking on.

She pushed open the gate. The path to the door hadn't been weeded and moss was thick on the paving stones giving the garden an air of neglect.

She felt in her bag for the key. It seemed strange opening this door — it made her feel almost like an intruder.

The hall was bare, with old bits of lino on the floor.

She walked hesitantly towards the kitchen.

Her heart sank. It was all so bare and unwelcoming. Bare spaces where the stove had sat, where the fridge had been. All bare and soulless.

She took her flask out of her bag and poured a cup of coffee. That was better. Now she could go upstairs. It would turn out fine, she kept saying as she went up the narrow flight of stairs. They creaked. She hadn't noticed that before.

The front bedroom was beige. There were squares of unfaded paper where the pictures had hung. It had a nice window, though. Quite large and with a built-in seat.

She sat for a moment looking out at the unkempt front garden. It would keep Peter busy all right. Still, he did seem keen to get started.

Enthusiastic was the better word. Peter was so enthusiastic over everything. He must think she was a proper wet blanket at times.

But she had loved the flat so much. She'd have been happy to stay there a little longer, while they took their time looking for a newer house. But Peter had persuaded her that this old house, with its nooks and crannies and large, wild garden with its ancient trees, was just the place to bring up his son. A little boy would have the time of his life there.

Dear Peter, so sure of everything. Even of the child she carried within her.

She smiled, and went into the back bedroom. This would be the nursery.

It was quite pretty — attractive in a chintzy way. The floor boards had been stained.

The bathroom had the biggest bath Cathy had ever seen. It was faced with solid mahogany. She smiled. Must weigh a ton. Still, it had charm, in a funny way.

Suddenly she remembered. Remembered the tree. The huge old plum tree in the garden.

Mrs Sanders had said what a wonderful tree it was. Cathy heard her bright voice again.

"My dear, this tree you wouldn't believe. Not all plum trees fruit every year. This one — well, it's laden. We've had loads of plums every year."

Cathy opened the kitchen door and went quickly out into the garden.

She ran over to the tree and looked up at the thick foliage. She couldn't believe her eyes.

It was empty of fruit. There wasn't a plum in sight.

She sank on to the rustic bench.

August was plum time. She'd had visions of herself in the kitchen bottling plums and making jam.

Slow tears began to trickle down her face.

Somehow this empty tree with its limp leaves was the last straw. She remembered all those dingy rooms in the house. Waiting to be painted.

"I wish we'd never set eyes on this house," she whispered savagely. "Why did we have to give up our flat to come here . . ."

GOOD afternoon." A man's deep voice made her jump. She looked across at the garden wall. An elderly man stood by it with a hoe in his hand.

She wiped quickly at her hot face.

"Oh, good afternoon," she mumbled.

"I'm Mr Maynard. Are you the new owner?"

She nodded. "Yes. I'm Mrs Lomax."

"Nice place you're moving into. May I say how pleased I am to see a young face. It's what we need round here, young people. We're all a bit set in our ways." He grinned.

He was nice, she decided.

"The house needs a lot doing to it," she said.

"Well, you'll cope. Young folk always do. Mr Sanders wasn't up to it," he replied.

A HOUSE OR A HOME

" The house is as sound as a bell, that's the important thing."

She rose and walked over to the wall.

"Oh, isn't your garden neat? We'll never get ours to look like that — it's so wild."

"Well, my wife liked everything just so. She's dead now but I daren't let things go. I reckon she'd come back and tell me to pull my socks up if I did," he said, and his eyes twinkled.

She looked over at the plum tree.

"Were the plums early this year?" she asked Mr Maynard.

"Oh, that tree. Well, now. I reckon they were, a few weeks maybe. Anyway, Mrs Sanders picked every one. She was a great one for bottling, you know. I expect she made full use of them before she left. I don't blame her — it's a wonderful cropper, that old tree. I've never seen another one like it and I've worked in gardens all my life."

"I see." Now it would be a whole year before they picked any fruit.

"Well," he said cheerfully, "must get on. Weeds wait for no man. Oh, tell your husband he's welcome to borrow any gardening tools he needs.

"It's not easy starting out. You'll find you need such a lot. Never mind, my dear, don't rush things."

"Don't rush things or you'll end up with everything you need and wondering where the years have gone."

He smiled again. "That's a bit of good advice from an old man."

"Thank you very much, Mr Maynard," Cathy said, trying to smile but finding it hard.

"Be seeing you then, my dear," he said, and disappeared into his garden.

Cathy sat back down on the bench. Perhaps it was tamable, this wild place. Peter would call it a challenge, but she felt too tired for challenges right now.

What a sight she must look. There was no water turned on in the house yet, so she couldn't even wash her hands or sponge her hot, dirty face.

WHEN Peter arrived home from work he found her still sitting in the garden.

"How's it going?" he asked anxiously.

"Oh, Peter, the plums have gone. Every one."

"Plums? Mrs Sanders must have picked them," he said.

"Mr Maynard said it was an early season. It *would* be."

"Who's Mr Maynard?" he asked, and tried to draw her close to him. She stiffened and he sighed.

"Our next-door neighbour. He said they were early. Laden it was, too. Like every year. Now we've got to wait a whole year before we get any," she complained.

"Well, Cath, it's not the end of the world. A few plums," he said practically.

Continued on page 162

The sweet smell of
AROMATHERAPY

Aroma-what? Well, it's basically the art of massaging away your ills with perfumed oils.

SINCE the days of Cleopatra and the Queen of Sheba, aromatic oils have been used to help relax and heal. Aromatherapy is the name of an ancient treatment using flower and herbal oils with massage.

The Elizabethans knew that various ailments could be helped by using herbal remedies. Among those well-known to our ancestors were oil of clarysage, rosemary and lavender to help with the problem of rheumatism. Lavender and marjoram were used for sleep problems, coriander for indigestion, camomile for migraine and eucalyptus for chest problems.

Once dismissed as 'Old Wives' Remedies', herbal medicines are now increasing in popularity as they are natural remedies giving relief and protection.

Some of the most popular oils are:

ROSEMARY — good for circulation, blood pressure and lowering of cholesterol levels, digestion, headache and migraine, arthritis.

ROSE — for depression, liver conditions, female conditions and as a tonic.

THYME — for colds, flu, throat and chest infections, as an antiseptic on skin.

JASMINE — for digestion, travel sickness, loss of appetite, rheumatism and arthritis, sprains.

PEPPERMINT — good for digestion, circulation and respiratory problems.

CAMOMILE — calming and soothing and suitable for childrens' complaints, female disorders, digestive troubles and allergies.

L

A HOUSE OR A HOME

Continued from page 160

Her eyes blazed. "You don't understand. That crop of fruit would have made things more bearable. Don't you see, this house would have been a home instead of just a dingy old place . . ."

Tears slid down her face once more.

"No. I don't understand, Cath," he said quietly, and she knew he was angry.

"All I know is that you've done nothing but look on the black side ever since we bought the house. Don't you trust me to make it good for you? I promised you I would, but it'll take time and I'll need help from you, not grumbles."

"But there's such a lot to do. Somehow, when I opened the front door today and saw empty places and dark paint I felt awful. Like standing at the foot of a slippery mountain," she said, and her voice wobbled.

"Empty houses are sad places, Cath," he said patiently. "But if we don't despair we'll manage. The main thing is that it's ours. Ours to do what we want with it. It's a challenge."

"I was waiting for you to say that," she retorted.

"What does that mean?" he asked, his eyes stormy.

Cathy sensed she was on dangerous ground and said quickly, "Come in and help me take measurements."

The front room was flooded by bright sunlight when they went inside.

"This is great," he said. "Make a lovely sitting-room. It'll be warm in here even in the winter."

He stood on the sill and held the tape measure up.

"Fade everything in sight, too," she muttered spitefully. Her head was pounding now.

"It's a shame the flat curtains won't be long enough for this room. Still, you'll soon run some new ones up, won't you?" he went on cheerfully.

My lovely curtains, she thought. They'll have to go upstairs.

"Bring any coffee?" he asked, jumping down.

"I did, but it'll be cold by now," she replied.

"Never mind, let's do the lot while we're here. We can have a drink somewhere on the way home."

SHE was measuring the window recess when Peter called to her from the kitchen. "Cath, come and have a look at this."

"What is it?" she asked, going through to the kitchen.

"Look here."

He was standing in front of a wooden wall cupboard. He swung the door wide.

"Just look," he said.

She gasped and stared in amazement. There on the shelves in neat rows were bottles of plums and jars of jam, all with dainty labels and blue and white checked covers. There was a card propped against a jar. She picked it up and read:

Just a welcome-in gift for you both. Thought you might enjoy some jam made with your own plums. Maybe you could spare a jar for Mr Maynard next door. Be happy here. Mr and Mrs Sanders.

"Well, Cath, feel better now?" Peter asked, and put an arm around her. This time she didn't draw away.

"What a kind thought," she said softly. "All that hard work. I don't deserve it. How awful I've been . . ."

"Not awful, darling, but perhaps a bit grumpy. Never mind, things will work out fine, I know they will," he said, and went over to where the old-fashioned sink stood with the wooden draining-board.

"Soon have this out," he said briskly. "One of those new units will make a world of difference."

She was still standing staring at the cupboard that was full of bottled fruit. There was all of summer ranged in rows there.

Dark red, gleaming jars on white, half-moon doyleys. They looked marvellous.

She felt the old house wrap around her then. A feeling of belonging crept through her. She was home.

"I don't want a unit, Peter," she said slowly. "Not just yet, anyway. After all, that old sink fits in perfectly with the rest of the house."

He shook his head. "I'll never understand women," he said. "Not if I live to be a hundred. I thought you wanted it all new and modern. I thought you couldn't wait for me to get rid of all this old stuff."

"So did I . . . before. Now . . . well, let's take our time. We mustn't be too anxious at first. That's a mistake. Mr Maynard said so."

She smiled at him and he smiled back.

"I must meet Mr Maynard," he said. "He seems to be quite a person."

"You will, right now," she replied. "We're taking him round some plums."

Before they closed the front door behind them, Peter said, "I do love you, Cath. I really do understand about you not wanting to leave the flat. I know how hard you worked to make it home for me, but we can do the same thing again here."

She kissed him.

"Of course we can. This is home now, darling. Now let's take these plums next door."

She turned at the creaky gate and looked back at the house.

The evening sun shone full on it. The windows were full of warm, welcoming light.

"We'll have to find a name for the house," she said as they closed the gate.

"That'll take time, too," he said. "When we've lived in it for a while then the name will come."

Then they went to give Mr Maynard the first fruits of their new home. □

A kiss for Santa

But she hadn't expected Santa to start kissing her back!

THE Toy Department of Wilson's wasn't quite the Christmas job I'd been hoping for, but believe me, I was only too glad to take it. That's one of the problems of living in a university town, there are so many students looking for jobs that you have to take what you can get.

So there I was, early in December, setting out every morning with my father. He liked to be in his office bright and early, so I was in town bright and early too. Even if it did mean getting up before I was awake.

Maybe that was the trouble that morning, a week after I started work. Maybe I wasn't quite awake.

Mrs Jones, in charge of Toys, was a pet, and she'd told me to slip off while things were quiet and have a cup of coffee. Take a chance, she said, before Mr Ward comes back.

I hadn't met Mr Ward. He was the Store Manager, and he was away on a business trip when I began work. I felt I knew him all too well before even meeting him, because I'd heard so much about him.

Very good looking, Mrs Simpson in Fashion said, but a cold fish. No sense of humour, Miss Bennett in Sportswear told me. Just let him catch you two minutes late, Mrs Norton of China warned me, and Miss Riley in Accessories added that only death or hospitalisation should ever keep me from work and Wilson's.

Mrs Jones said he wasn't that bad, it was just that he was young for his responsibilities, and he felt he had to take his job seriously. But she's the kind of person who always sees the best in other people. Not in a sloppy way, she just sees their good points instead of their bad points.

Anyway, because Mrs Jones is that kind of person, it bothered me,

165

when I came back from my coffee, to see how down she was. She's small and plump, and usually smiling, but today there was no smile.

The store was quiet, so we had a chance to talk. She told me that she was so worried about her little granddaughter. The doctor thought she had a heart murmur, and she was having tests done to find out. I tried to cheer her up, but it wasn't easy.

As I say, maybe it was because I wasn't quite awake that I did such a stupid thing. We had some funny faces on one of our stands, and I lifted a clown's face, with a big red nose, and put it on. Then I did a little clown act for her. Trying to cheer her up, you see.

It was working, too. There was the beginnings of a smile on her face, and I gave an extra skip on the strength of it.

Then I saw the smile freeze, and she was looking over my shoulder. I began to feel a little cold, and I turned round.

I think I knew who he was right away. He was wearing a dark suit, and he had horn-rimmed glasses on. They were right, he was good looking, with dark hair, dark eyes and one of these lean brown faces.

"Mr Ward," I said faintly, but I don't think he heard me properly, with the mask over my face.

He came right up to me, and lifted my clown mask aside. For a long time he looked at me, unsmiling, and I felt my heart sink and my face grow scarlet.

"Miss Carter, I presume," he said in a scarlet voice that dripped ice. "Our student helper. I'm glad to see that you feel so thoroughly at home in our Toy Department."

He handed me my clown mask, and stood watching while I put it back on the shelf. Then, with a sort of regal inclination of his head, he turned and left us.

"You're for it, Penny," Mrs Jones warned me. "He'll be watching you, to see how you behave." She shook her head. "I wish I'd known he was coming back today, but I don't think anyone did."

Anyway, I told myself, I'd managed to cheer her up a bit, and later in the day she had a phone call from her daughter to say that all the tests showed the heart murmur was nothing to worry about.

Wilson's is quite a big store, and Mr Ward was responsible for the whole place, but somehow, wherever I went, I seemed to see him.

The day I knocked over my cup of coffee in the staff canteen, he happened to be walking past our table, and he only just escaped. Actually, a drop or two of coffee did spill on his beautiful shoes, but I wasn't going to point that out to him.

And the time my mother phoned to tell me the cat had had her kittens, I came down the escalator two at a time, to tell Mrs Jones.

"If you were a nurse, Miss Carter, I'd presume there was an emergency," Mr Ward said, as we both kind of spilled off the escalator at the bottom. "But since you're not, I think you'll find that the speed of our escalator is quite adequate for any crisis that might arise in the store. Do you agree?"

I said he was quite right, it was just that I wanted to tell Mrs Jones about the kittens.

"She wants one for her granddaughter's birthday in January, you see," I explained. "And we were so worried in case they mightn't be proper Siamese, because Sheba did get out, and we didn't know if it was after or before her proper mating, and they promised Angie a Siamese kitten."

Mr Ward looked a little dazed.

"And they are proper Siamese," he guessed.

"Oh yes. Mum says they're perfect."

"I am not in the least interested in your cat's love life," he told me coldly. "If it's not asking too much, Miss Carter, perhaps you could do a little work now and again."

"But — " I began to protest angrily. It was too late. He'd already turned and started to walk away. I stuck my tongue out at his back. It seemed to be the only way I could think of to relieve my feelings.

A FEW days before Christmas, I was in trouble again. There was this little boy, you see, about seven or eight years old, and he wanted to buy a glove puppet of Snoopy for his little sister, but he didn't have quite enough money. We counted it twice over, he and I, and he was still twenty pence short.

"I'm sorry," I said, and I really meant it. "Should I put it aside for you, and maybe you can get more from your mother?"

"She can't give me any more," he told me, quite matter-of-factly. "Not with Dad away from us, you see. Have — have you something else my little sister would like, please?"

I showed him a plastic teaset, and then a skipping-rope, but he kept looking back at Snoopy.

He was too bright to deceive, and he'd seen the price sticker, so I couldn't say I'd made a mistake.

"I'll put in the twenty pence," I told him.

His face lit up.

"Sometimes I get money for Christmas," he said, after a moment. "I could pay you back later."

I was going to say it didn't matter, but I could see that it did matter to him, and so I agreed that he could pay me later, and wrapped up Snoopy for him. He had just walked away, his parcel in his hands, when I looked up and saw Mr Ward there.

"I'd like to see you in my office, Miss Carter," he said brusquely.

I swallowed, and went over to tell Mrs Jones where I was going.

I'd never been in Mr Ward's office before, and his secretary told me he was on the phone, but just to go in. So I knocked and went in.

Mr Ward was leaning back in his chair, and he had his glasses off. He looked quite different, I thought, surprised. Then he saw me, and he straightened up.

"Sorry, Joan, I'll let you know later," he said quickly. "What? Yes, Friday night as usual." He put the phone down.

"You wanted to see me?" I asked.

He reached for his glasses and put them on. Now he looks like a

A KISS FOR SANTA

Samuel, I thought, and without them he should just be called Sam. Not, of course, I told myself hastily, that I was likely ever to call Mr Ward either Samuel or Sam.

"I think you know why, Miss Carter," he said.

I nodded.

"You can't do that, you know. We'll have all the kids for miles around coming in and giving you a hard-luck story."

"It wasn't just a hard-luck story. Mr Ward," I told him earnestly. "It was true."

"I'm sure it was," he replied. "But — you must remember that we're running a business here."

"Even businesses can have hearts," I said stubbornly. "It was only twenty pence, after all."

"I know it was only a small amount," he agreed. "But you're setting a precedent, Miss Carter, so — don't do it again."

Our Santa Claus arrived the next day. He was from the Pensioners' Home nearby, and he was round and roly-poly, and just right for being Santa Claus. I had to help him get ready, and tie his red robe on him, because he had difficulty managing the ties, being so rotund.

I loved seeing him with children, he was so sweet with them, especially the smallest ones. He told me that this was what he missed most of all in the Home, seeing children.

He needed the money he earned, but it was a long day for him, and sometimes when it was quiet in the morning, Mrs Jones and I would put up the "Santa Will Be Back Soon" notice, and give him a cup of tea in his little grotto.

WE knew that Christmas Eve was going to be frantic, and that had to be the day the white poodle came in.

Mrs Jones saw him first, trotting up and down the aisles in a business-like, interested way, wagging his tail whenever anyone spoke to him, getting under people's feet. We managed to catch him, and saw that he had no disc on his collar, to tell us where he lived.

Just then it got busy, and when I looked up, I saw the girls from Cosmetics chasing him out of the main door and into the street.

"You can't do that," I told them as I ran out after him. "He'll be run over — we'll have to take him to the police station."

Sure enough, he was standing at the edge of the busy road looking at the traffic flashing past. Any moment he would have run out on to the street, and not only got himself run over, but probably caused an accident too. I grabbed him, and went back into the store.

"I suppose I'll have to look after him," I told the Cosmetics girls, and I took him back to Toys. I'd take him to the police station in my lunch-hour. I told Mrs Jones, and she said fine, but what were we going to do with him until then?

There was only one place for him — in Santa's Grotto, hidden by the voluminous red robes of Santa himself. Forturnately, the poodle was only too pleased to co-operate. He settled himself down, and all our Santa had to do was to reach back for the Lucky Dip parcels, without really moving or disturbing the poodle.

This worked well, until halfway through the morning, Mr Ward came to see if we needed any more Lucky Dip parcels.

"No, we're all right," I told him quickly, heading him away from the grotto. "We have plenty, and if we need any more I'll get them."

"I'll just look and see," Mr Ward said firmly, and he walked nearer. I was sure I could hear sounds from the dog, but fortunately the store was pretty busy and noisy.

Mr Ward asked our Santa how he was, and if he wasn't finding it too tiring, and the heat of the robes and beard didn't bother him. Before I would have been pleased to hear this evidence that he was human, now I just wanted him to move away.

He did after about five minutes that felt like five hours. Mrs Jones and Santa and I all breathed sighs of relief, and relaxed. But half an hour later Mr Ward was back again, this time carrying more Lucky Dips for us.

"I knew you'd run short of them," he told us, "we always do."

There was nothing Santa could do but stand aside. Mr Ward put the bundle of parcels down, and there was the dog, looking up at him and wagging its tail as if it had found a long-lost friend.

"Miss Carter," Mr Ward said indignantly. "I presume you know something about this?"

I explained about the dog being likely to be run over, and I told him that I intended taking it to the police station in my lunch hour, and I pointed out that he wasn't bothering anyone.

"In the first place. Miss Carter," Mr Ward pointed out, in his turn, "you aren't going to have more than a ten-minute lunch hour today. You'll have to take over in Fashion in your lunch hour, we're short there. And in the second place, it's setting a precedent. We can't keep stray animals in the store."

He picked the white poodle up, and bundled it under his arm.

"I'll get someone to take him to the police station," he told me.

By lunch-time, the shop was frantically busy. Mrs Jones was alone in Toys, and I had to help in Fashion while Mrs Simpson dashed upstairs for a quick sandwich. There was a lady on the point of buying one of the expensive imported dresses from Israel, she said, all I had to do was finalise the sale.

I went to the cubicle where the customer was, and asked if I could come in. A voice said I could.

My customer was looking at herself in the mirror. She was built on what my father calls generous lines, and the dress she was trying on wasn't meant for ladies like her. Oh, it fitted, but it didn't make her look any smaller.

In the mirror, our eyes met.

"Mrs Simpson said it was just right for me," she said uncertainly.

Charitably, I tried to think that Mrs Simpson was in a hurry, and not that she was thinking of her Christmas Eve Target. I'd helped out in Fashion before, and thinking quickly I could come up with two or three dresses that would look much, much nicer on this lady. But all at least half the price.

I looked down at my feet, unable to meet the customer's eyes any longer. I tried to tell myself that it wasn't really my business, all I had to do was finalise the sale. And then I thought of my customer wearing her dress over Christmas and New Year, and not looking as nice as she could look. And knowing it, I lifted my head.

Once again, our eyes met in the mirror. I shook my head.

"I've got a couple of dresses that will look much nicer on you," I told her, and I went off to get them.

She chose the casually-tailored one I'd been sure would look nice on her, and when she went away she was smiling. But Mrs Simpson wasn't smiling when I had to explain to her what I'd done. And Mr Ward wasn't smiling, either, when he sent for me later.

"No doubt you have a very good reason for losing Mrs Simpson's sale, Miss Carter?"

"Yes, I have."

And I explained. "Surely," I said when I'd finished, "It's better for the reputation of Wilson's to send out a satisfied customer, Mr Ward?"

"Oh yes," he agreed. His eyes met mine, levelly. "But Mrs Simpson seems to feel that this customer was reasonably satisfied until you put doubts into her mind."

I thought about this, and I had to be honest.

"If I'd said it looked fine she would have gone off quite happily. But I couldn't do that, because I knew she could look so much nicer. And she did."

Mr Ward shook his head.

"All right, we'll leave it there for the present. I'm sure you're busy in Toys and I have no time to give you a lecture."

THE year before, I hadn't had a Christmas job because my mother had been ill, and I'd been looking after things at home.

This was my first experience of Christmas Eve in a big store, from the salesgirls' point of view. And it was frantic. People were making their minds up in a hurry, and coming back half an hour later because they'd had another think. I kept running up and down to the storeroom, to get things we were short of.

Fortunately for our poor old Santa, things quietened down in the late afternoon, and there were hardly any children coming to his grotto. Not long before closing time, as I hurried back from another trip to the storeroom, I realised with dismay that the poor old man had hardly had a break.

He was sitting patiently outside his grotto, and my heart went out to him.

Mrs Jones was busy with a customer, so I went right to the grotto.

"Come on, Santa," I told him firmly — we always called him Santa, never Mr Harris, just in case there were any children around. "You must be worn out. I'll put the notice up, you slip inside and put your feet up, and I'll bring you a cup of tea."

He started to say something, but before he did I stopped him.

"And don't worry about Mr Ward — he'll never know. He's never found us any of the other times, has he?"

Without waiting for an answer, I bundled him back into the grotto, and hurried off to get him a cup of tea from the canteen, nice and strong, the way he liked it.

He took the tea and drank it, with only a muttered "thank you." And suddenly I guessed what was wrong with him. I knelt on the floor beside him.

"You're sad at the thought of this finishing, aren't you?" I said, softly. "Because you've loved being with the children."

Because I'd become so fond of him in the time he'd spent with us, I got up and put my arms around him, and kissed his cheek.

For a moment, I had a bewildering confusion of sensations. A cheek that was surprisingly firm, a faint smell of after-shave lotion, an arm that was unbelievably strong. And then Santa's beard slipped, and I realised that I was kissing Mr Ward's cheek.

"Mr Ward!" I gasped. "What are you doing here?"

"Giving Santa a rest," Mr Ward told me.

Then his beard came off completely, and he was kissing me very thoroughly. And very pleasantly.

"Mr Ward," I said again, faintly. "You're setting a precedent, you know."

He let me go, and burst out laughing.

"So I am," he agreed. And still with his arms around me, he asked me when I was leaving the store.

"Next week."

"Thank heaven for that," he said, in such heartfelt tones that my heart sank.

He looked down at me. "Because while you're here, it's almost impossible for me to concentrate as I should on my job," he told me, smiling cheerfully. "And speaking of that, I have to go now and see about closing up for the day — I thought poor old Santa was tired out."

He handed me the white beard and the red robe.

"We close in half an hour," he reminded me. "I'll be waiting to take you home. Any objections, Miss Carter?"

I shook my head. "None at all, Mr Ward," I assured him meekly.

And then, just to make it quite clear, I said it again: "None at all, darling." □

Fancy That!

She was quiet and shy, but she discovered she could really make a party go with a swing!

IT had been that kind of a day. Emma had hardly known whether she was coming or going. The telephone never stopped ringing. Her boss kept changing his mind during dictation and even now she was typing one letter for the third time.

She had no break for lunch. Her head was beginning to ache, and now, of all people, Malcolm Greig had just telephoned to ask her to a fancy-dress party on Friday evening.

Her headache almost forgotten, Emma sat back in a small glow of pleasure, tinged slightly with apprehension. She put the receiver down and thought about Malcolm's invitation.

For three years, she had stood on the fringe of Malcolm Greig's social world, too quiet, too shy and too insecure to make any step or overture towards him, even though she thought he was the most kind, most unassuming and easily the most handsome young man in the whole of Parkbridge.

He commuted daily from his parents' comfortable suburban villa to a good job in an accountant's office. He always smiled when he saw her, but the mere thought that he might speak evaporated Emma's courage.

173

FANCY THAT!

"For heaven's sake give me some ideas," Emma pleaded. "There must be something simple but startling."

Morning after morning, Emma fled, flushed and confused, to another compartment. Now, wonder of wonders, he had telephoned and asked her to a party. And it was a fancy-dress one at that . . .

"I'm still not sure about the second paragraph," said Mr Jackson, suddenly looming at the side of her desk.

"I think it's perfect, just perfect," Emma said, already miles away, wondering how the Queen of Sheba wore her hair.

At first, the prospect of a fancy dress party had dismayed her. Then, on quick reflection, Emma realised it could be a blessing in disguise. She did not have any really fashionable party clothes.

But fancy dress was another matter altogether. She needed an outstanding and spectacularly brilliant idea. Something that would make her stand out in the crowd. She did not want to merge with a gathering of gypsies or be passed over in a crowd of pirates. She wanted to be admired, noticed and applauded for her ingenuity, especially by Malcolm.

In the next few days, she went through and discarded at least a dozen ideas from Madame Pompadour to Wonder Woman. It had to be within her ability to put together, to sew, to concoct from whatever was handy.

"For heaven's sake, give me some ideas," Emma pleaded with her mother. "There must be something simple but startling."

"How about wearing your pretty tiered skirt and putting a ribbon on your dad's walking stick and going as a shepherdess?"

Emma groaned. "Oh no, not a shepherdess. Who's going to notice a shepherdess? I'd be about as outstanding as that old standard lamp."

"Why not go as a standard lamp?" her father suggested, letting his glasses slip down his nose and peering over the top of them. "We'll lend you the shade. Add a bit of fringe round the edge."

"That's not funny," Emma said. "I don't want to look an idiot."

"Besides, she's not tall enough," her mother added.

B Y Friday morning Emma still had not decided what to wear to the party. She had washed her long hair till it shone, golden, burnished. She had painted her nails a new shade of pink. Mr Jackson even let her go home early.